HOW
YOUR
LIFE
INSURANCE
POLICIES
ROB
YOU

This book has been credited with achieving the very purpose Arthur Milton intended when he authored it ten years ago—to create a more competitive atmosphere in the life insurance industry and enable consumers to gain increased financial security. The predecessor to this 1990 edition of *How Your Life Insurance Policies Rob You* has been through 72 printings and can be found in most libraries across the country. We estimate that over 4 million readers have read the book and benefited from its message. Now, in 1990, we are again proud to introduce the revised, updated version of *How Your Life Insurance Policies Rob You.*

THE PUBLISHER

ARTHUR MILTON

HOW YOUR LIFE INSURANCE POLICIES ROB YOU

ALL NEW EDITION

A CITADEL PRESS BOOK
PUBLISHED BY CAROL PUBLISHING GROUP

Manufactured in the United States of America
ISBN 0-8065-1176-1

10 9 8 7 6 5 4 3 2 1

Dedication

There is an inherent irony in that the phrase life insurance actually represents a means of preparing for death. It's one way to make certain outstanding loans or unsettled business agreements are favorably resolved. And most important, it can protect a family when—in the natural order of things—the head of the household is no longer there to care for them.

And it is bitterly ironic that, as I was writing this book, I had to confront the idea head-on—not the death of a father or mother, or uncle, or brother, but the death of my youngest daughter, Patricia Ann.

It is to Pat I dedicate this book. To Pat, who loved life and all living things—who "collected" unwanted animals and neglected children, and captivated all who knew her with her loving spirit and generous heart.

When Pat died on May 7, 1980, at the age of 23, I realized a somber truth: You can protect your family for all the tomorrows through financial security, but the greatest legacy is your time and your love today . . . and each day that you live.

Above all, those were the gifts I wanted to leave my Patricia. As it happened, things did not happen in their natural order. With Patricia's untimely death these gifts were, instead, her legacy to me.

I am a far richer man for them.

Acknowledgments

I am grateful:

To my many friends in insurance and the other professions, who over the years have contributed to my knowledge, views, enthusiasms, and philosophies.

To my many clients who have taught me much about human wants, needs, and behavior.

To the millions of people who became my friends after the initial publication of this book in June of 1981. Many have thanked me by mail, phone, and in person for the help they received so that they, too, might live in dignity, retire in dignity and, if need be, die in dignity.

A.M.

Publisher's Foreword

IN 1981, if Arthur Milton could have seen into the future, perhaps he would have been prepared for the incredible reaction to his book *How Your Life Insurance Policies Rob You* when it first appeared in bookstores. While Mr. Milton had no way of predicting the phenomenal response, one thing he did know was his own mind.

He knew he was angry, angry at his own industry, the life insurance industry, in which he had spent his entire career. He knew that he could no longer stand back quietly and ignore the abuse that was taking place every day in homes all across America, the injustices that continued only because the traditional insurance industry had tricked and cajoled the American public into thinking that their so-called "professional" agents knew what was best for them and their families. The continued abuses of a callous industry could no longer be tolerated, and Mr. Milton could no longer stand silent. It was time to expose those injustices, and with the writing of this book, Mr. Milton set about on a one-man campaign to expose the frauds and abuses of the life insurance industry.

Actually, there were two reactions, entirely separate and very different. The good news was that readers responded to the book en masse. Mr. Milton's exposé of one of the largest and most powerful industries in the world—the life insurance industry—confirmed many of the suspicions that consumers had had all along about the shifty-eyed agent who showed up at their door threatening doom and gloom and offering security at a premium price. Many people smelled something fishy in the exorbitant cost of life insurance, and Arthur Milton told them that their noses were perfectly "in joint."

The consumer response was outrage, but it was the best kind—outrage mixed with action. By the hundreds of thousands, consumers took Mr. Milton's advice to heart and responded by cancelling over-priced, overblown products and replacing them with cheaper term life insurance that allowed for maximum death protection for minimum dollars.

The other response was not quite as pleasant. The traditional life insurance industry, caught naked by Mr. Milton with little defense for its actions, screamed bloody murder. Since the publication of the book, Mr. Milton has been the victim of many attacks by insurance industry executives, general agents and insurance organizations. He has been exposed to criticism in the media by an industry who saw the monopoly it had ruled for over one hundred and fifty years starting to crumble. Caught without a viable means of explanation for the practices that Mr. Milton exposed, and panicked by the threat to their pocketbooks, many people throughout the industry chose to attack. Robust disagreement is an inherent part of the American way. But often, the attacks Mr. Milton has received have gone beyond spirited disagreement. Faced with such conditions, many people would have withdrawn the book, if only to avoid the unpleasantness and live a more peaceful life. Many would have gladly let it fade away and tried to distance themselves from the controversy.

But that has not happened. Not only has Arthur Milton stood by his original material, he has made frequent updates. In addition, he has made himself available as a speaker and lecturer, accepting over a thousand television, radio and newspaper interviews. In short, he has not shied away from, but actively promoted, the contentions formed during what is now forty-five years in the life insurance and financial services industries. He has vigorously pursued the opportunity to educate consumers on the right and wrong ways to buy life insurance.

It's been almost nine years since *How Your Life Insurance Policies Rob You* was released, and it remains the backbone of the consumerist movement in life insurance in America today. The controversy the book set off nine years ago has, no doubt, been responsible for at least part of the success of that movement. In the ensuing nine years, the insurance industry has changed dramatically. While many of the old abuses continue, many companies have been forced to acknowledge the power of the consumer. Some have gone out of business; many others have lost tens of thousands of clients as consumers became aware of alternatives to traditional cash value life insurance. Hundreds of articles have appeared touting the virtues of term insurance, lobbying for more consumer-oriented legislation of the industry, lambasting abuses of the establishment companies—in other words, the same messages that Arthur Milton sent out in this book nine years ago. More agents have been themselves educated, and some have crossed over to the term insurance camp. Term life insurance companies have enjoyed amazing successes.

It must be gratifying for Mr. Milton to see the action

in the industry today, and to know that he had some part in propagating it. It is gratifying for us, as publishers of *How Your Life Insurance Policies Rob You*, to continue to be a part of a publishing venture that has played a significant role in reforming an industry.

As we go to press yet again, we continue to revel in the fact that this book is being used extensively to help people understand life insurance and other money matters and to play a role in the financial security and financial independence of many American families.

Contents

For a hundred and fifty years the life insurance establishment has cheated Americans by concentrating on selling high-priced whole life policies instead of providing death insurance at a reasonable cost . . . The life insurance industry has become a voracious octopus, squeezing the financial life's blood out of millions of American families. But this is one evil the individual can do something positive about.

The 1979 report of the Federal Trade Commission staff that cash value life insurance returned an average of only 1.3 percent to policyholders in 1977 poses a showdown threat to the tradition of only state regulation for life companies . . . Congress may be ready to return responsibility of the insurance industry back to the FTC.

xv

*The apathy of most state regulatory officials. We don't
have a Charles Evans Hughes now . . . The power of
insurance lobbies in state capitals . . . The difficulty in
getting outstanding insurance commissioners . . . State
officials don't live up to the recommendations of their own
professional association.*

4.   The Confession/47

*The gradual impact of the confidential 1979 Trend Report
of the Institute of Life Insurance, which concluded that
the business is on a "self-destruct course." This document
is a tacit confession that the life companies long have
grossly overcharged their customers. It may be fifteen
years old, but it is more true today than ever.*

5.   Typical Abuses/57

*A typical life insurance story and high-pressure mail-order
selling . . . Conglomerate bottom-line perils . . . Scare selling: Who needs cancer insurance? . . . TV ads.*

6.   Double Dipping in Credit Life/65

*One-third of the annual premium collections on credit life
insurance probably represents overcharges, and to add
insult to injury, the borrowing consumer has to pay high
interest on the premium. A fight looms in Congress to end
this abuse.*

11. The Industry's Mistakes/107

The unjustified mystique . . . Wasteful children's insurance . . . Too many rogues . . . The policy-loan-interest racket . . . Poor agent selection and training . . . Unjust restrictions on policy replacements.

12. The Disclosure Fiasco/119

The industry's poor public image . . . Deliberate deceptions . . . The widows study . . . The NAIC disclosure-plan hoax . . . Failure of the huge public relations effort to tell people what they need to know.

13. Life Insurance: Are You Robbing Yourself?/127

Life insurance in a nutshell . . . Keep it simple . . . Financial planning taboo . . . You need a Ph.D. to help you buy term insurance and invest the difference . . . The universal life policy sham . . . Wounding the octopus.

14. The Heart of the Matter/155

Combining term insurance and assorted other investments . . . The agent as a "money doctor" . . . Varieties and costs of term life insurance.

Preface

THIS BOOK WAS WRITTEN IN ANGER, an anger accumulated gradually over forty-five years as a practicing insurance agent, insurance broker, and stockbroker trading principally in insurance company stocks.

Its purpose is to stir people to action on their own behalf and to help them gain financial security.

A secondary purpose is to generate debate in the insurance industry to cause action that will benefit our population, which is so dependent on insurance.

A large amount of information about the predatory, autocratic, and sometimes criminal activities of the life insurance establishment is widely known to many persons active in the business and to some educators, regulatory officials, and politicians. I have remarked in previous books about some of the industry's greedy absurdities. Over the past twenty years, other authors and government reports have painted in the details of the ugly picture. The Institute of Life Insurance's 1974 *Trend Report*, circulated confidentially among the top brass of the industry establishment, admitted the truth of virtually all the accusations against the industry you will read about in this book. Of course, the *Trend Report* made these admissions in a very back-handed, self-righteous way, but the report reached the then-startling conclusion that the life insurance industry was on a "self-destruct course" if it continued to operate as it has for the past century, with its huge emphasis on selling costly whole life cash value policies.

This conclusion, I am sure, was not reached without realizing that today even the life insurance industry is dealing with a consumer movement that was nonexistent only twenty years ago. If the insurance industry doesn't act more vigorously and prudently to clean its house, consumerist leaders like Ralph Nader will do it for them. The education in recent years of our population in money matters, including insurance, cannot and should not be underestimated by the insurance industry and the regulators. In addition, the inflationary spiral has caused the average person to seek a dollar's value for a dollar spent even in buying death (life) insurance.

Getting back to the *Trend Report*—self-destruction for whom or for what? Certainly not for the basic principle of life insurance, which is financial protection for the survivors when a family breadwinner dies. Neither Americans nor any other people are going to give up that great social benefit achieved over the past two hundred and fifty years.

No, the self-destruction will be that of the predatory and hypocritical people who control and manage the establishment life insurance companies, pursing selfish, high-handed policies to delude millions of people and swindle them out of their earnings and savings. The impact of concentration of financial power in the life insurance octopus on the national economy is evil and corrupting. Many life insurance companies have corrupted representatives in Congress, many state legislators, and state regulatory officials in order to serve their privileged position and to keep the unsophisticated public from knowing about their duplicity and plundering.

Like most other insurance agents, I acquired this knowledge slowly. The first company I worked for gave me a training course that amounted to deliberate brainwashing. Necessarily, I sold some policies in my younger years I wouldn't dream of recommending today, but they were the best available to me then, just as wooden boats, which are subject to rot and require painting, caulking, and other costly maintenance, were the best available then to boat buyers. Now virtually all boats are made of fiberglass, which doesn't rot and requires virtually no maintenance. The establishment life companies have improved their products the way boat builders have, to meet the competition of the day. *They have not righted the longstanding wrongs to the older policyholders.*

But I am glad to say that I began opening my eyes rather early. I quickly realized the absurdity of such cruel hoaxes as the endowment policy, and I was still very young when I became outraged by the racial, religious, and sex discrimination toward both applicants for insurance and job hunters of the establishment companies. I was a pioneer in crying out against the folly of selling burdensome cash value insurance to young people instead of inexpensive term insurance that provides genuine protection to survivors. But it took me longer to accept the fact that, in spite of all the benefits life insurance has conferred, the industry establishment has become a colossal monster that must be torn down and completely rebuilt. For example, the waste of policyholders' money not only on inflated salaries, but on grandiose architecture for home offices to feed the egos of top management, should be relegated to the past.

I was not alone in the industry in rebelling against its abuses and injustices. A number of other life insurance executives and agents and some regulators of the industry have spoken out over the years against the abuses and excesses complained of in this book. These courageous people will not regret the appearance of this book, because its indictment does not pertain to them. Some of them have had to pay with their jobs for their efforts to bring out the truth, but they have persisted. This kind of criticism from within the profession is needed more than ever today by the insured public.

So, as in the case of many other economic and social abuses, the individual American is not helpless in the face of the sins of the life insurance establishment. If he or she will take some time to study the matter, enough companies can be found that are eager to sell death protection at reasonable cost and on fair terms, and there are enough independent agents with sufficient sophistication and integrity to help them—companies and agents who foresee the future in this age of consumerism and want to serve the policy buyer, not swindle her or him.

But what about the tens of millions who are too unsophisticated and too apathetic to mend matters on their own? Should the life insurance predators continue to be allowed to gouge them mercilessly? No!

I can only hope that the two hundred thousand plus captive life insurance agents in America are becoming as sensible and sensitive as I have become to the injustices of the establishment companies. But I suspect many of them will feel they would be risking their jobs by being caught with a copy of this book.

In any event, we certainly should not continue to tolerate the corruption and domination of so much of our

economy and government by the greedy and arrogant rul-
ing clique of the insurance establishment.

Arthur Milton

*P.S. This book was written in 1980 and early 1981, and
much has happened since then to benefit the insurance-
buying public. Yet, in 1989, there are more assaults on
the consumers' dollars than ever before. Therefore, I have
updated much of this material, and I have added two
new sections, a chapter on the AIDS scare and a concluding chapter which provides an updated analysis and over-
view of the issues in this book.*

Introduction

THE ONLY THING THAT IS CONSTANT IS CHANGE. This cliché is well-known by those who recognize that decade after decade the progress of our country and the progress of our world have often meant constant change, particularly in the sphere of economics as it pertains to each and every individual. Frankly, for decades I have felt that the term *life insurance* is a misnomer. I now feel the time has come to do away with this misnomer and call it what it is, *death insurance.*

We call financial protection against flames fire insurance and protection against loss by overflowing streams flood insurance, and the various parts of a comprehensive automobile insurance policy are known by the perils protected against. So why not call protection against the hazard of death by its right name? I suspect the misnomer *life insurance* arose because of the dread of death and the taboo against talking too much about it in an age more superstitious than ours. But *life insurance* is an absurd label, and the term *living insurance* being promoted by one large establishment company is even more farfetched. (However, since *life insurance* is so widely used and is even part of the names of many companies, I have used the term throughout this book, to avoid confusion.)

People should protect their loved ones, their business properties, their outstanding loans, and their business agreements with proper death insurance, and the result should be maximum protection for minimum premium outlay.

Now that we've established what life insurance (or death insurance, as I would prefer) *is*, let me make clear what it is *not*. It is *not* a savings account, it is *not* a college fund for the kids, it is *not* an investment vehicle. In today's economic climate, it is absolutely absurd in most cases to continue to use an insurance policy (such as the traditional whole life cash value insurance) for any of these purposes or to consider purchasing one that uses these purposes as a selling point.

Also, the need for you to consider a much greater amount of death (life) insurance than you probably have is certainly clear.

Finally, after having advised tens of thousands of clients over the past four and a half decades to purchase the right kind of insurance, other consumer advocates and government officials, as well as many of those in the life insurance industry, now have sided with my philosophy and my theories on financial planning.

As you read through the following pages, you will find important information that makes it absolutely necessary for you to start an immediate review of your *death insurance* needs and also to consider appropriate areas in which to invest your capital so that you may have adequate financial security in your twilight years.

HOW
YOUR
LIFE
INSURANCE
POLICIES
ROB
YOU

1. *The Voracious Octopus*

For a hundred and fifty years the life insurance establishment has cheated Americans by concentrating on selling high-priced whole life policies instead of providing death insurance at reasonable cost . . . The life insurance industry has become a voracious octopus, squeezing the financial life's blood out of millions of American families. But this is one evil the individual can do something positive about.

WE AMERICANS are going through the most frustrating period of our national history since the Civil War, but there is one serious evil every one of us can help overcome.

We are encompassed by a sea of troubles, mostly of our own making but some resulting from the malice, envy, and bigoted fanaticism of other peoples throughout the world, peoples whom we have tried to befriend but

1

have succeeded only in making into enemies. At home we
are beset by a persistent serious inflation (13.4 percent in
1980, fortunately reduced in 1989 to 5 percent).

We have not been able to cope with falling productivity in our industries, an apparent breakdown of much
of our school system, appalling crime, and a moral and
social convulsion with the drug culture most of us cannot
even comprehend, much less cope with.

We have been humiliated in Iran. and our national
conscience over the war in Vietnam will be a continuing
canker to us for generations to come.

These frustrations are doubly bitter to the individual
American, because he or she can do nothing about any of
these terrible evils. Only concerted national opinion and
action, guided by determined leadership. can have the
slightest effect.

The evil we all can do something about immediately
has been going on for a hundred and fifty years, and the
majority of Americans are extremely reluctant to recognize it and wipe it out, although it has extracted from
millions of persons billions of dollars. It has cruelly
hoaxed most of the population and has created a predatory financial debacle the scale of whose deceptive and
avaricious practices makes those of organized crime, and
nearly all the other greedy and oppressive commercial and
industrial rackets of the past, seem petty.

With forty-five years of a close relationship with the
insurance industry, I feel obliged to tell my readers my
observations in the strongest terms possible, as well as
relating my concerns. Fortunately, these broad-brush
accusations apply to only a few. By and large, those serving the insurance industry are honorable persons and, I
am convinced, can and will change the climate for the

betterment of our entire population, which is dependent on an honest insurance industry.

The perpetrators of this evil, which we all have the ability to elude and erode if we will, are the most hypocritical rascals ever seen in this country, with the possible exception of the more scandalous religious charlatans of today and the nineteenth-century patent-medicine barons. Today's charlatans are the life insurance companies, who sell millions of overpriced and almost useless cash value policies to persons who, instead, desperately need adequate, sensibly-priced financial protection for the survivors when the family breadwinner dies.

The reluctance of the American public to accept the fact that the life insurance establishment has been operating a monstrous and cruel racket for generations is natural enough. People think about life insurance with gratitude because it did provide a means, albeit a grossly inadequate means, of fending off starvation and homelessness in the wake of the vast social upheaval caused by the industrial revolutIon and the military and political revolutions that accompanied it.

Although the life insurance industry is nearly two hundred and fifty years old, it grew very slowly in the first century for two fairly obvious reasons. To many millions it seemed an unfeasible idea because human life then was so uncertain and mortality rates were so high. This made it an unattractive business to the hardheaded eighteenth-century and early-nineteenth-century financiers. The other reason was that it seemed unnecessary in an age when society in much of the world, even in the industrialized countries. was still stratified and feudal and most people had a place in life tied in some way to the land. People had roots in the land on which they could depend. The nobility and the rich landholders were obligated by law, custom, and religion to care for the widow and children of a tenant, serf, or employee who died. They had to make a place for these dependents and give them at least the bare necessities of life. Therefore the populace, which was semiliterate at best, was slow to appreciate the idea of life insurance.

The erosion of feudalism in England began in Tudor times, with the first enclosure movements that drove some peasants off the lands their forehears had farmed for generations. The industrial revolution and the new enclosure movements in England and Scotland in the eighteenth century, when landlords uprooted hundreds of thousands of tenants and sharecroppers to make room for sheep grazing, finished off the remnants of British feudalism. The same thing happened on the continent of Europe. The world's millions became indeed the world's dispossessed. They no longer had roots and a place on the land to which they had a hereditary right to return or a lord or landlord who owed them succor.

Life insurance began to make sense. But it still was not easy to sell, and it was even more difficult to get insured persons to keep up their policies and pay premiums. Also, in both Europe and the United States, the young industry encountered many frauds on the part of applicants for insurance. Medical examinations were falsified, and insured persons, particularly children, were murdered in large numbers to collect on the policies. In an age when most parents could reasonably expect two out of five or even more of their offspring to die of childhood maladies, an astonishing number of couples saw nothing wrong in exploiting this fact to defraud the insurance companies. So, historically speaking at least, not all the wrong has been on the part of the companies. But the life insurance companies responded to these abuses by writing tough, even very tricky, clauses into the policies designed to prevent fraud by insured persons and their beneficiaries. Indeed, they put in so many restrictive clauses that the business began to get a bad reputation, and selling policies became even more difficult.

Then someone thought of cash value, realizing that this "savings" feature could become a most potent sales tool, a great inducement to insured persons to keep up their policies, and an excuse for raising premiums sharply. It is doubtful that the insurance men who first launched the cash value policy realized what an enormous bonanza it would turn out to be by increasing the sales volume of high-priced whole life policies to a golden flood. But it wasn't long before smart financiers saw the immense possibilities, got into the business, and began to milk the public—and they have been doing it ever since.

So we see that cash values were not a part of the original life insurance concept; in fact, very soon after they were introduced, thoughtful critics began to condemn the whole idea. The first published criticism appeared in the United States in 1868. The critics pointed out that cash values did nothing but raise the cost of death protection for the insured's survivors. They also saw correctly that the so-called savings feature of cash value in life insurance policies was a hoax because the savings were not added to the death benefit and, in the long run, rarely amounted to nearly as much as the policyholder had paid in.

Even at that early date and in that era of relatively low interest rates and stable currencies, sober voices were raised warning the public that the only real function of life insurance was the financial protection of survivors and that life insurance never could be anything but an inferior investment instrument.

Although whole life insurance was the original concept, sophisticated buyers with high purchasing power were rather quick to see how expensive it really was. Ultimately these sophisticates negotiated deals for large amounts of life insurance on fixed, renewable terms at greatly reduced premium prices that went up with each renewal. But few companies got into this business, and those that did kept it so in the dark that their own agents did not know about it for many years. So much pressure was exerted on agents to keep this term insurance business secret that it was almost never mentioned in public.

So for more than a century, enormous pressure was put on insurance agents to concentrate on selling expensive cash value policies. This pressure continues virtually unabated today. It was achieved mainly by making the commission schedule on cash value insurance so much more attractive than the commissions on term insurance that many agents felt they could not afford to recommend modestly-priced term insurance to customers. Indeed, for a long time, the agents were so ill-trained and so rigorously indoctrinated that millions of them took as gospel the representations of the companies that whole life and cash value were what was really best for their customers.

It takes only a minute's reflection to understand why cash value insurance has to be overpriced and provide vastly less protection than term insurance. Fundamentally, an insurance company, when it writes a policy, makes a wager that the insured will not die soon. The odds for this wager are set on the basis of mortality experience.* The younger the policy buyer is, the longer

---

*See Mortality Table, pages 8-9.

odds the company can afford to give in the form of low premiums; the older the policy buyer. the shorter the odds and the higher the premiums. Whole life insurance policies have an element not found in any other usual type of wager; every one of us must die eventually, so the insurance company must pay the bet—unless the policy lapses. As a matter of fact, a very high percentage of whole life policies do lapse, and the company gets whatever has been paid in premiums and the policyholder loses his or her wager outright. Unlike the horseracing bookmakers and other professional gamblers who take wagers from the public, the life companies calculate their odds so they make money on virtually every individual policy even though they have to pay off a great many of their wagers. The only time the company loses is when an insured person dies soon after taking out the policy. But even these losses are much more than offset by the large number of policies that lapse. On these, no death benefit ever has to be paid.

In practice, rates have been set higher than really necessary, so the difference between the cost of term insurance in the younger and middle years and of whole life insurance is staggering. The harsh truth is that the average family can buy from five to ten times as much insurance protection for a dollar in term policies as in whole life cash value insurance. Life rates are complicated, depending on many factors such as age, health, the amount of insurance bought, various policy options, and the term of the policy. Thus, there is a wide range in the amounts of term and whole life insurance a dollar will buy.

It is axiomatic that the bigger the unit prices and mark-ups of what it sells, the more profitable an efficiently run business is in terms of percentage return on

MORTALITY TABLES

| | Commissioners 1980 Standard Ordinary (1970-1975) | | | | 1983 Individual Annuity Table (1971-1976)* | | | | United States Population (1979-1981) | |
| | Male | | Female | | Male | | Female | | | |
Age	Deaths Per 1,000	Expectation of Life (Years)	Deaths Per 1,000	Expectation of Life (Years)	Deaths Per 1,000	Expectation of Life (Years)	Deaths Per 1,000	Expectation of Life (Years)	Deaths Per 1,000	Expectation of Life (Years)
0	4.18	70.83	2.89	75.83	—	—	—	—	12.60	73.88
1	1.07	70.13	.87	75.04	—	—	—	—	.93	73.82
2	.99	69.20	.81	74.11	—	—	—	—	.65	72.89
3	.98	68.27	.79	73.17	—	—	—	—	.50	71.93
4	.95	67.34	.77	72.23	—	—	—	—	.40	70.97
5	.90	66.40	.76	71.28	.38	74.10	.19	79.36	.37	70.00
6	.86	65.46	.73	70.34	.35	73.12	.16	78.37	.33	69.02
7	.80	64.52	.72	69.39	.33	72.15	.13	77.39	.30	68.05
8	.76	63.57	.70	68.44	.35	71.17	.13	76.40	.27	67.07
9	.74	62.62	.69	67.48	.37	70.20	.14	75.41	.23	66.08
10	.73	61.66	.68	66.53	.38	69.22	.14	74.42	.20	65.10
11	.77	60.71	.69	65.58	.39	68.25	.15	73.43	.19	64.11
12	.85	59.75	.72	64.62	.41	67.28	.16	72.44	.25	63.12
13	.99	58.80	.75	63.67	.42	66.30	.17	71.45	.37	62.14
14	1.15	57.86	.80	62.71	.43	65.33	.18	70.46	.53	61.16
15	1.33	56.93	.85	61.76	.44	64.36	.19	69.47	.69	60.19
16	1.51	56.00	.90	60.82	.45	63.39	.20	68.49	.83	59.24
17	1.67	55.09	.95	59.87	.46	62.42	.21	67.50	.95	58.28
18	1.78	54.18	.98	58.93	.47	61.44	.23	66.51	1.05	57.34
19	1.86	53.27	1.02	57.98	.49	60.47	.24	65.53	1.12	56.40
20	1.90	52.37	1.05	57.04	.51	59.50	.26	64.55	1.20	55.46
21	1.91	51.47	1.07	56.10	.53	58.53	.28	63.56	1.27	54.53
22	1.89	50.57	1.09	55.16	.55	57.56	.29	62.58	1.32	53.60
23	1.86	49.66	1.11	54.22	.57	56.59	.31	61.60	1.34	52.67
24	1.82	48.75	1.14	53.28	.60	55.63	.33	60.62	1.33	51.74
25	1.77	47.84	1.16	52.34	.62	54.66	.35	59.64	1.32	50.81
26	1.73	46.93	1.19	51.40	.65	53.69	.37	58.66	1.31	49.87
27	1.71	46.01	1.22	50.46	.68	52.73	.39	57.68	1.30	48.94
28	1.70	45.09	1.26	49.52	.70	51.76	.41	56.70	1.30	48.00
29	1.71	44.16	1.30	48.59	.73	50.80	.42	55.72	1.31	47.06
30	1.73	43.24	1.35	47.65	.76	49.83	.44	54.75	1.33	46.12
31	1.78	42.31	1.40	46.71	.79	48.87	.46	53.77	1.34	45.18
32	1.83	41.38	1.45	45.78	.81	47.91	.48	52.80	1.37	44.24
33	1.91	40.46	1.50	44.84	.84	46.95	.50	51.82	1.42	43.30
34	2.00	39.54	1.58	43.91	.88	45.99	.52	50.85	1.50	42.36
35	2.11	38.61	1.65	42.98	.92	45.03	.55	49.87	1.59	41.43
36	2.24	37.69	1.76	42.05	.97	44.07	.57	48.90	1.70	40.49
37	2.40	36.78	1.89	41.12	1.03	43.11	.61	47.93	1.83	39.56
38	2.58	35.87	2.04	40.20	1.11	42.15	.65	46.96	1.97	38.63
39	2.79	34.96	2.22	39.28	1.22	41.20	.69	45.99	2.13	37.71
40	3.02	34.05	2.42	38.36	1.34	40.25	.74	45.02	2.32	36.79
41	3.29	33.16	2.64	37.46	1.49	39.30	.80	44.05	2.54	35.87
42	3.56	32.26	2.87	36.55	1.67	38.36	.87	43.09	2.79	34.96
43	3.87	31.38	3.09	35.66	1.89	37.43	.94	42.12	3.06	34.06
44	4.19	30.50	3.32	34.77	2.13	36.50	1.03	41.16	3.35	33.16
45	4.55	29.62	3.56	33.88	2.40	35.57	1.12	40.20	3.66	32.27
46	4.92	28.76	3.80	33.00	2.69	34.66	1.23	39.25	4.01	31.39
47	5.32	27.90	4.05	32.12	3.01	33.75	1.36	38.30	4.42	30.51
48	5.74	27.04	4.33	31.25	3.34	32.85	1.50	37.35	4.88	29.65
49	6.21	26.20	4.63	30.39	3.69	31.96	1.66	36.40	5.38	28.79
50	6.71	25.36	4.96	29.53	4.06	31.07	1.83	35.46	5.89	27.94
51	7.30	24.52	5.31	28.67	4.43	30.20	2.02	34.53	6.42	27.10
52	7.96	23.70	5.70	27.82	4.81	29.33	2.22	33.59	6.99	26.28
53	8.71	22.89	6.15	26.98	5.20	28.47	2.43	32.67	7.61	25.46
54	9.56	22.08	6.61	26.14	5.59	27.62	2.65	31.75	8.30	24.65
55	10.47	21.29	7.09	25.31	5.99	26.77	2.89	30.83	9.02	23.85
56	11.46	20.51	7.57	24.49	6.41	25.93	3.15	29.92	9.78	23.06
57	12.49	19.74	8.03	23.67	6.84	25.09	3.43	29.01	10.59	22.29
58	13.59	18.99	8.47	22.86	7.29	24.26	3.74	28.11	11.51	21.52
59	14.77	18.24	8.94	22.05	7.78	23.44	4.08	27.21	12.54	20.76

MORTALITY TABLES (cont'd.)

	Commissioners 1980 Standard Ordinary (1970-1975)				1983 Individual Annuity Table (1971-1976)*				United States Population (1979-1981)	
	Male		Female		Male		Female			
Age	Deaths Per 1,000	Expectation of Life (Years)	Deaths Per 1,000	Expectation of Life (Years)	Deaths Per 1,000	Expectation of Life (Years)	Deaths Per 1,000	Expectation of Life (Years)	Deaths Per 1,000	Expectation of Life (Years)
60	16.08	17.51	9.47	21.25	8.34	22.62	4.47	26.32	13.68	20.02
61	17.54	16.79	10.13	20.44	8.98	21.80	4.91	25.44	14.93	19.29
62	19.19	16.08	10.96	19.65	9.74	20.99	5.41	24.56	16.28	18.58
63	21.06	15.38	12.02	18.86	10.63	20.20	5.99	23.69	17.67	17.88
64	23.14	14.70	13.25	18.08	11.66	19.41	6.63	22.83	19.11	17.19
65	25.42	14.04	14.59	17.32	12.85	18.63	7.34	21.98	20.59	16.51
66	27.85	13.39	16.00	16.57	14.20	17.87	8.09	21.14	22.16	15.85
67	30.44	12.76	17.43	15.83	15.72	17.12	8.89	20.31	23.89	15.20
68	33.19	12.14	18.84	15.10	17.41	16.38	9.73	19.49	25.85	14.56
69	36.17	11.54	20.36	14.38	19.30	15.66	10.65	18.67	28.06	13.93
70	39.51	10.96	22.11	13.67	21.37	14.96	11.70	17.87	30.52	13.32
71	43.30	10.39	24.23	12.97	23.65	14.28	12.91	17.07	33.15	12.72
72	47.65	9.84	26.87	12.28	26.13	13.61	14.32	16.29	35.93	12.14
73	52.64	9.30	30.11	11.60	28.84	12.96	15.98	15.52	38.82	11.58
74	58.19	8.79	33.93	10.95	31.79	12.33	17.91	14.76	41.84	11.02
75	64.19	8.31	38.24	10.32	35.05	11.72	20.13	14.02	45.07	10.48
76	70.53	7.84	42.97	9.71	38.63	11.13	22.65	13.30	48.67	9.95
77	77.12	7.40	48.04	9.12	42.59	10.56	25.51	12.60	52.74	9.44
78	83.90	6.97	53.45	8.55	46.95	10.00	28.72	11.91	57.42	8.93
79	91.05	6.57	59.35	8.01	51.76	9.47	32.33	11.25	62.77	8.45
80	98.84	6.18	65.99	7.48	57.03	8.96	36.40	10.61	68.82	7.98
81	107.48	5.80	73.60	6.98	62.79	8.47	40.98	9.99	75.52	7.53
82	117.25	5.44	82.40	6.49	69.08	8.01	46.12	9.40	82.78	7.11
83	128.26	5.09	92.53	6.03	75.91	7.57	51.89	8.83	90.41	6.70
84	140.25	4.77	103.81	5.59	83.23	7.15	58.34	8.28	98.42	6.32
85	152.95	4.46	116.10	5.18	90.99	6.75	65.52	7.77	107.25	5.96
86	166.09	4.18	129.29	4.80	99.12	6.37	73.49	7.28	117.12	5.61
87	179.55	3.91	143.32	4.43	107.58	6.02	82.32	6.81	127.17	5.29
88	193.27	3.66	158.18	4.09	116.32	5.69	92.02	6.38	137.08	4.99
89	207.29	3.41	173.94	3.77	125.39	5.37	102.49	5.98	147.28	4.70
90	221.77	3.18	190.75	3.45	134.89	5.07	113.61	5.60	158.68	4.43
91	236.98	2.94	208.87	3.15	144.87	4.78	125.23	5.26	171.69	4.17
92	253.45	2.70	228.81	2.85	155.43	4.50	137.22	4.94	185.70	3.93
93	272.11	2.44	251.51	2.55	166.63	4.24	149.46	4.64	200.23	3.71
94	295.90	2.17	279.31	2.24	178.54	3.99	161.83	4.37	214.95	3.51
95	329.96	1.87	317.32	1.91	191.21	3.75	174.23	4.12	229.76	3.34
96	384.55	1.54	375.74	1.56	204.72	3.51	186.54	3.88	243.38	3.19
97	480.20	1.20	474.97	1.21	219.12	3.29	198.65	3.65	256.37	3.05
98	657.98	.84	655.85	.84	234.74	3.07	211.10	3.44	268.68	2.93
99	1,000.00	.50	1,000.00	.50	251.89	2.86	224.45	3.22	280.30	2.82
100					270.91	2.66	239.22	3.01	291.20	2.73
101					292.11	2.46	255.95	2.80	301.99	2.64
102					315.83	2.26	275.20	2.59	310.89	2.57
103					342.38	2.08	297.50	2.38	319.70	2.50
104					372.09	1.90	323.39	2.18	327.86	2.44
105					405.28	1.73	353.41	1.98	335.39	2.38
106					442.28	1.57	388.11	1.79	342.33	2.33
107					483.41	1.41	428.02	1.60	348.70	2.29
108					528.99	1.27	473.69	1.43	354.53	2.24
109					579.35	1.13	525.66	1.26	359.88	2.20
110					634.81	1.01	584.46	1.11		
111					695.70	.89	650.65	.97		
112					762.34	.78	724.75	.83		
113					835.06	.70	807.32	.71		
114					914.17	.67	898.89	.60		
115					1,000.00	.50	1,000.00	.50		

Note: Mortality rates contained in the 1980 Commissioners Standard Ordinary Table were obtained from experience of 1970-1975, but contain an added element designed to generate life insurance reserves of a conservative nature in keeping with the long-term guarantees inherent in life insurance contracts. Premiums for life insurance policies, on the other hand, are based on assumptions that include expected mortality experience.

Mortality rates for the 1983 Individual Annuity Tables are, again, conservative as related to the actual and projected experience upon which they are based.
*Projected to 1983.

ANNUAL PREMIUMS FOR $100,000 INSURANCE

TRAVELERS INSURANCE COMPANY

Male Age 35 - Face Amount 100,000

Age	Yr	Annual W/L Prem	W/L Death Benefit	C/V per 1,000	20 yr Term Prem	+Diff to Invest	Side Fund 12%	Term, Death Benefit
35	1	1,176	100,000	0	210	966	1,081.92	100,000
36	2	1,176	100,000	600	210	966	2,293.67	100,000
37	3	1,176	100,000	1,300	210	966	3,650.83	100,000
38	4	1,176	100,000	1,900	210	966	5,170.85	100,000
39	5	1,176	100,000	2,500	210	966	6,873.27	100,000
40	6	1,176	100,000	3,600	210	966	8,779.98	100,000
41	7	1,176	100,000	4,700	210	966	10,915.50	100,000
42	8	1,176	100,000	5,800	210	966	13,307.28	100,000
43	9	1,176	100,000	6,900	210	966	15,986.32	100,000
44	10	1,176	100,000	8,100	210	966	18,986.32	100,000
45	11	1,176	100,000	9,400	210	966	22,346.60	100,000
46	12	1,176	100,000	10,700	210	966	26,110.11	100,000
47	13	1,176	100,000	12,000	210	966	30,325.24	100,000
48	14	1,176	100,000	13,300	210	966	35,046.19	100,000
49	15	1,176	100,000	14,700	210	966	40,333.65	100,000
50	16	1,176	100,000	16,200	210	966	46,255.61	100,000
51	17	1,176	100,000	17,700	210	966	52,888.21	100,000
52	18	1,176	100,000	19,200	210	966	60,316.71	100,000
53	19	1,176	100,000	20,700	210	966	68,636.64	100,000
54	20	1,176	100,000	22,300	210	966	77,954.96	100,000
55	21	1,176	100,000	23,700	210	966	88,626.67	0
56	22	1,176	100,000	25,100	210	966	100,578.99	0
57	23	1,176	100,000	26,500	210	966	113,965.58	0
58	24	1,176	100,000	27,900	210	966	128,958.56	0
59	25	1,176	100,000	29,300	210	966	145,750.70	0
60	26	1,176	100,000	30,600	210	966	164,557.90	0
61	27	1,176	100,000	32,400	210	966	185,621.96	0
62	28	1,176	100,000	34,000	210	966	209,213.71	0
63	29	1,176	100,000	35,600	210	966	235,636.47	0
64	30	1,176	100,000	37,200	210	966	265,229.96	0

Due to the miracle of compound interest, my age 35 example is
well on the road to self insurance having accumulated $77,954.96
at the end of twenty years. At each year prior to that the
protected family would have two accounts in the event of death.
The 100,000 death benefit and the side fund.

It is easy to see that the next twenty years from age 55 to 64
the miracle really works developing your side fund to $265,229.96.

ANNUAL PREMIUMS FOR $100,000 INSURANCE

Premium - 11.56
Policy fee - 20.00

Male Age 35 - Face Amount 100,000

Age	Yr	Annual W/L Prem	W/L Death Benefit	C/V per 1,000	*20 yr Term Prem	+Diff to Invest	!Side Fund 12%	Term Death Benefit	#Total
35	1	1,176	100,000	0	210	966	1,081.92	100,000	101,081.92
36	2	1,176	100,000	600	210	966	2,293.67	100,000	102,293.67
37	3	1,176	100,000	1,300	210	966	3,650.83	100,000	103,650.83
38	4	1,176	100,000	1,900	210	966	5,170.85	100,000	105,170.85
39	5	1,176	100,000	2,500	210	966	6,873.27	100,000	106,873.27
40	6	1,176	100,000	3,600	210	966	8,779.98	100,000	108,779.98
41	7	1,176	100,000	4,700	210	966	10,915.50	100,000	110,915.50
42	8	1,176	100,000	5,800	210	966	13,307.28	100,000	113,307.28
43	9	1,176	100,000	6,900	210	966	15,986.32	100,000	115,986.32
44	10	1,176	100,000	8,100	210	966	18,986.32	100,000	118,986.32
45	11	1,176	100,000	9,400	210	966	22,346.60	100,000	122,346.60
46	12	1,176	100,000	10,700	210	966	26,110.11	100,000	126,110.11
47	13	1,176	100,000	12,000	210	966	30,325.24	100,000	130,325.24
48	14	1,176	100,000	13,300	210	966	35,046.19	100,000	135,046.19
49	15	1,176	100,000	14,700	210	966	40,333.65	100,000	140,333.65
50	16	1,176	100,000	16,200	210	966	46,255.61	100,000	146,255.61
51	17	1,176	100,000	17,700	210	966	52,888.21	100,000	152,888.21
52	18	1,176	100,000	19,200	210	966	60,316.71	100,000	160,316.71
53	19	1,176	100,000	20,700	210	966	68,636.64	100,000	168,636.64
54	20	1,176	100,000	22,300	210	966	77,954.96	100,000	177,954.96
55	21	1,176	100,000	23,700	**210	966	88,391.48	**26,578	114,969.48
56	22	1,176	100,000	25,100	210	966	100,080.37	23,916	123,996.37
57	23	1,176	100,000	26,500	210	966	113,171.93	21,563	134,737.93
58	24	1,176	100,000	27,900	210	966	127,834.48	18,476	146,310.48
59	25	1,176	100,000	29,300	210	966	144,256.53	16,719	160,975.53
60	26	1,176	100,000	30,600	210	966	162,649.23	14,440	177,089.23
61	27	1,176	100,000	32,400	210	966	183,249.05	12,586	195,835.05
62	28	1,176	100,000	34,000	210	966	206,320.85	11,494	217,814.85
63	29	1,176	100,000	35,600	210	966	232,161.27	9,313	241,474.27
64	30	1,176	100,000	37,200	210	966	261,102.54	8,529	269,631.54

  * Term is a level premium for 20 years.
  ** Convert to Decreasing Term Insurance after twenty years
    continuing to spend $210.00 a year on insurance.
  # Death Benefit plus Side Fund.
  + Annual Whole Life premium minus 20 year Term premium.
  ! Difference to Invest compounded at 12% annually.

Due to the miracle of compound interest, my age 35 example is
well on the road to self insurance having accumulated $77,954.96
at the end of twenty years. At each year prior to that the
protected family would have two accounts in the event of death.
The 100,000 death benefit and the side fund.

It is easy to see that the next twenty years from age 55 to 64
the miracle really works developing your side fund to $261,102.54.

sales. This is the basic profit bonanza the establishment life insurance industry has succeeded in building and maintaining for a century in the United States and Europe.

For many years the establishment companies were not satisfied with even these huge premium profits. So they introduced a hybrid called the endowment policy and sold it as if it were manna from heaven. This was a deal under which the sucker paid on the policy for twenty, thirty, or forty years, then could cash it in for a little better amount than the cash value of whole life or trade it for a small annuity payable until death. The trouble with this little beauty was that it provided only one-thirtieth to one-tenth as much death protection for the money as term insurance.

Life insurance companies take the money you pay in premiums and invest it in stocks and bonds or lend it. They reap rather handsome profits on these investments for many years. The income is kept on the books in a separate account from premium income, but it all goes toward the overall profit on the company's shares if it is a stock company. Many of the big establishment life companies are mutuals. In theory, they are owned by their policyholders and pay dividends on the policies instead of dividends on stock. Most critics of the mutual companies contend that these dividends are in the main only a return of a small amount of the excessive premiums the mutual companies charge on whole life policies, sometimes as much as thirty percent more than the charges of stock life companies. The U.S. Internal Revenue Service apparently agrees with this position. It never has sought to tax the dividends on mutual life insurance policies as profit or income. Neither does the government tax the policy dividends paid on "participating" policies issued by stock life insurance companies. It taxes only dividends paid directly on their shares.

In general, the life companies have historically had excellent returns on invested capital as well as high returns on sales. Until the mid-1960's, there were many instances in which you could have invested as little as ten thousand dollars in a life company, and it would have appreciated through stock splits and stock dividends until the original ten thousand dollars had become perhaps five hundred thousand dollars.* However, the life insurance stock market peaked in 1964, and there have been fewer bonanzas in recent years. Still, life insurance is far from a capital-intensive business. It runs on money collected from policyholders and its investments, not on the sale of new securities or borrowings, as other businesses do. The big multi-line companies do have a lot of stock in the hands of the public, but much of it was issued as stock dividends or to pay for the purchase of other insurance businesses. Very little was sold for cash.

Nevertheless, most life insurance companies have big sales volumes in proportion to their invested capital. So when they reap a high yield on policy premiums and a high yield on capital they are profiting doubly at the expense of the public—to a degree that few businesses have been able to do without resorting to monopolistic practices. The truth is that most businesses that have high sales volumes in proportion to invested capital— supermarket chains, for example—have to content themselves with very small yields on sales, perhaps only two percent, and be satisfied with a respectable yield on

---

* See Arthur Milton, *Life Insurance Stocks: The Modern Gold Rush* (Secaucus. N.J.: Citadel Press. 1963).

capital. If such businesses seek too high a yield on sales, they become uncompetitive.

Like policy dividends, the cash value accumulations under whole life insurance policies are not profit, although many insurance agents pretend they are and the companies do little to dispel the illusion. Again the proof that these accumulations are not profit but only a partial repayment to the policyholder of the excessive premium he or she has been charged is that the Internal Revenue Service has so ruled and never has sought to tax cash value payments as profit or even as income. A warning: If cash surrender values and dividends eventually exceed the total amount of premiums paid in over the years, the excess can become taxable income. This sometimes happens.

By now some readers may imagine I want Congress to outlaw cash value life policies and the courts to start sending insurance company executives and agents to jail for selling them. Not true. While I personally could never recommend cash value in any of its forms, particularly the newest variety, universal life, I maintain an unbridled faith in the free enterprise system as the only workable system for a free society. In order to preserve that system, we must allow the freedom of individual—and companies—to market whatever product they choose, and let that product live or die based on how it is received by consumers in the marketplace. At the same time, however, it is my part of this freedom (and my personal and professional obligation) to speak out against what I consider to be an unsound concept and product and against the many abuses I see within the cash value life insurance industry.

In my opinion, the reality of the situation is that it is

virtually impossible to find a modestly priced, dividend-paying whole life cash value policy that will provide death protection more cheaply in the long run than a level death benefit term policy for the same amount at the same age. To further confuse matters, the financial comparisons usually presented in support of such claims for whole life insurance are hard for the layperson to comprehend and are based on dividend assumptions that are only guesses, since the dividends are not guaranteed.

Whole life policies are widely used in the special field of business life insurance, which includes partnership insurance and key-man protection. A partnership policy protects the surviving partner or partners from the financially unpleasant consequences of the death of one partner. Key-man insurance provides money to tide a business over the trying days following the death of its active head or any other key people. Whole life insurance has been sold in this field by agents who make big commissions on it on the plea that it alone can meet the high health risks in business—for example, a heart attack striking a partner—and that renewing term insurance in such circumstances would be difficult or at least very expensive. The argument is also advanced that cash values are useful in business life insurance because there is always the possibility that something might happen that would make it desirable to terminate the insurance and recover some of the premium. However, many insurance people, including me, believe that judicious use of the right kind of term insurance can be cheaper and just as efficient in solving business life insurance problems.

Of course, the galloping inflation that has engulfed the American economy in recent years has forced us all to face up to the consequences of the whole life rip-off.

Inflation has eroded the prospective death benefit of the small whole life policy we bought many years ago until it hardly seems worthwhile to continue to pay premiums on it. Wouldn't it be better to cash it in and put the money in a savings bank or in some other investment that pays reasonably good interest or in stock that pays dividends?*

This situation has created a problem for the insurance industry, a problem the life insurance trade press calls "the replacement crisis." Many insurance agents are either persuading their customers to replace their old policies with newer ones that offer more protection and better cash and dividend values—or with packages of term insurance and such outright investment instruments as annuities and mutual funds—or they are yielding to the customer's pleas for such help. This sort of thing flies right in the face of the philosophy of the establishment companies. It is plain heresy, and they are filling the insurance trade press and the general press, when they can, with exhortation to people to hang on to their old policies no matter how bad they are. Also, it comes as rank insubordination on the part of the agents; how dare these upstarts put their customers' needs ahead of the sacred privileges of the establishment fat cats?

Writing in the *National Underwriter* for December 1, 1979, Richard K. Carter, a vice president of New York Life Insurance Company, quoted Calvin Coolidge. whose penny-pinching and ever-backward-looking policies brought on the great depression of the 1930's, as urging people In a radio talk in 1931 not to let anyone persuade them to switch their policies "without the best advice of the companies that issued them. . . . If you let someone

---

*See Arthur Milton, *Will Inflation Destroy America?* (Secaucus, N.J.: Citadel Press, 1977).

switch you, he will surely make money, but you will probably lose." Cautious Cal was a director of New York Life at the time. Carter opined that Coolidge's remarks were valid for today.

Hogwash! The American people are starting to disagree most emphatically, and a few rare, progressive, consumer-oriented companies that have seen the advantages of replacing something bad with something better are starting to make a serious dent in the old-guard philosophy that replacement is a sin within the insurance Industry.

To life insurance people, one of the most criminal aspects of the current inflation is that, in effect, it makes life insurance seem worthless to persons in their late sixties or seventies unless they are quite well off. Most ordinary folk that old cannot afford the high premiums of term insurance in those brackets even if they are still physically insurable, and the whole life policies they bought years ago have been rendered almost worthless by inflation. The death benefit of many of these policies won't exceed six months' or a year's Social Security benefits. A really small whole life policy may not even pay for a decent funeral. Social Security provides a burial benefit, but it isn't much. To prove my point. in 1987 the average size death claim of all life insurance companies in the United States was a paltry $7,050!*

The revolt against whole life cash value insurance abuses is already well advanced. As a matter of fact. better than seventy percent of all life insurance in force in the United States is term insurance.To my friends in the industry who will think I took this fact out of my hat, I

*See Arthur Milton, *Who's Right for the American Consumer?* (New York, N.Y.: Timely Publications, 1988).

suggest they simply add up the individual term policies, group insurance, credit life insurance, association term policies, etc. The American people and the agents have forced this change. But the greater part of the term insurance still is not written by the big establishment companies or even by the many smaller conventional companies. It is written by companies that have seen the wave of the future.

That doesn't mean that the struggle is won or is necessarily going to be won without a big effort. The greater amount of premium income in the business, and particularly the premium income of the establishment companies, comes from whole life cash value insurance by far, and that's the way the establishment companies want to keep things. *What is being bought today does not offset the bad impact on the public of the costly cash values or even high-cost term policies sold in the past.*

As a matter of fact, premium rates have been reduced so drastically in the past few years that almost all policies issued prior to January 1, 1989, can be replaced at better rates with less cost to the consumer.

The sins of the establishment life companies do not end with abuse of whole life cash value policies. Throughout much of the industry's history they have operated on outdated mortality tables that enable them to inflate their rates and rig the odds of the insurance wagers in favor of the companies and against policyholders and beneficiaries.

For years they discriminated against women and racial minorities unconscionably, penalizing females unjustly and outrightly denying insurance to blacks. They rule their agents with a tyrannical hand and have brought extreme pressure against independent agents to prevent the dissemination of information about the realities of life insurance economics and to preserve the fictitious gospel that their predatory policies are necessary and just.

The companies have also achieved enormous financial power: They became as potent as the banking establishment as a source of funds for equity and loan capital for business and other segments of the national economy. They used this financial power ruthlessly, to influence legislators and regulatory officials so the companies could protect their selfish interests. Thus, this voracious octopus spreads its tentacles ever wider, to suck blood and treasure from the American people. They even succeeded in getting amendments tacked onto federal laws, forbidding some government agencies to oppose their ruthless policies.

I am chagrined and even embarrassed at many of my colleagues who are behaving in such an unprofessional manner—after all, they will have to accede eventually to the current needs of the people they serve. I am concerned that the many insurance associations that I was a member of for forty years cannot see the forest for the trees in this ever-changing world.

Nevertheless, in the long run, the life insurance establishment was not able to prevent sensibly priced term insurance from being made available to the general public through independent companies and independent agents. Since about 1950, sensible, reasonably-priced term insurance has been available. Term insurance rates in the year 1989 are so low and so available that no growing family in America should be without at least $100,000 to $250,000 of death insurance protection.

Even though this is all true, it has not stopped these big companies and their armies of agents from continuing

to mislead the public and sell people unsuitable policies at
high prices. It has not stopped their flood of false propaganda about the great virtues of cash value insurance,
and it has not stopped their effort to prevent or delay the
spread of truthful information about life insurance companies.

The confused situation is aggravated by the attitude
of the establishment life companies that anyone outside
their own official family who presumes to write or talk
about life insurance is guilty of prejudice and ignorance
and is telling malicious lies in an effort to tear down a
sacred institution. They are particularly incensed when
members of Congress such as Senator Howard Metzenbaum, government bodies such as the Federal Trade
Commission, or academic economists specializing in
insurance present caustic analytical pictures of the industry and its products. They accuse the critics of having political or at least self-serving motives.

Considering all the political shenanigans that many
investigations in our national history have revealed on the
part of the establishment life insurance companies, and
considering the huge lobbies they maintain in Washington
and every state capital, it is downright comical for the
insurance establishment to call the FTC and the academic
economists politically biased and self-serving.

Just what can individual Americans do to overcome
the voracious life insurance octopus? The answer is simple: Just be very careful about buying life insurance. Find
out about it. Information is available. Ever since Herbert
Denenberg (who moved from a professorship at the
University of Pennsylvania's Wharton School to become
the state's insurance commissioner) published *The
Shopper's Guide to Life Insurance* and circulated two

million copies of it, eye-opening information has been available. Denenberg bluntly urged Congress to outlaw cash value insurance unless the companies came up with an honest and adequate program of pricing-information disclosure. He also charged that eighty percent of the companies were "suspect" and that forty percent of all agents were incompetent.

In the years since the first appearance of the Denenberg guide, New York and several other states have published similar guides. So it is manifest that no one has to be victimized by a life insurance company any longer.

However, no matter how honestly and carefully they are prepared, these official guides to buying life insurance are not easy reading. It takes a lot of time and a natural aptitude or long experience at research to digest them. Articles in such publications as *Changing Times* and other consumer magazines stick more to general principles with fewer cumbersome details, but they still leave the uninitiated pretty puzzled.

In other words, you still need an agent. The question is, What kind of agent? Here are some rules for choosing one:

• Don't select an agent just because he or she is a relative or neighbor. Check the agent for competence. Don't regard a big sales volume as the prime indicator— that could indicate just an unscrupulous huckster.
• When you chose an agent you still have to check him or her out carefully. If the agent seems in a hurry to get your check and signature on the application, show him or her to the door and look for someone more interested in your personal needs. Agents also sell annuities or mutual funds and fortunately for you they do not

have to make a maximum commission on the sale of life insurance that's unsuited for you.

The New York State Insurance Department gives some additional rules:

• Ask friends, relatives and business associates to recommend agents.
• Talk with him or her. If you don't feel that an agent cares about your personal needs, find another one.
• Make sure an agent explains the costs and coverage of everything fully.
• Try to decide if he or she is the kind of person you can depend on to keep you posted about changes in available coverages and other opportunities. A lazy agent can really hurt you.
• Make sure she or he isn't the kind of rip-off artist who, under the pretext of reviewing your situation, will sell you new policies no better than those you have, just to generate commissions.
• Above all, don't fall for the "professional insurance agent" who emphasizes his professionalism. Even in the medical profession those unscrupulous surgeons who have performed hysterectomies and heart operations in the last few decades are now coming under question as to just how many of these operations were necessary. Latest reports that I read indicate that anywhere from twenty-five to fifty percent of these patients could have lived as well, or better, without the operation. So before you sign up for an operation on your checkbook, get that second, and even third opinion before you act.

Even these fairly simple rules aren't easy to follow,

but I can give you one rule that is easy to follow, and since more persons buying life insurance for the first or second time are relatively young, it applies to most people. Here it is:

Life insurance is really death insurance. The first con-sideration in buying it, the only real consideration is to provide maximum financial protection for surviving family members if the breadwinner is killed or dies of illness. In these days when both husband and wife often have jobs, such protection may be needed against the death of both spouses. A survivor of either sex is in a devil of a spot today if he or she loses a spouse and has children to bring up.

The basic rule is, truly, maximum dollar protection for minimum cost.

2. Time For Federal Intervention

The 1979 report of the Federal Trade Commission staff that cash value life insurance returned an average of only 1.3 percent to policyholders in 1977 poses a showdown threat to the tradition of only state regulation for life companies . . . Congress may be ready to return responsibility of the insurance industry back to the FTC.

FOR TWO AND A HALF YEARS the Federal Trade Commission wrestled with the problem of working out a better way to show consumers how to find out just how good or bad a life insurance policy is.

The long effort resulted in a 455-page report published in the midsummer of 1979. Its conclusions startled, even stunned, people who didn't know much about life insurance and enraged some industry leaders. The report said that the average return to policyholders on whole life cash value insurance was only 1.3 percent in 1977. The FTC staff added that life insurance policyholders would have received $3.7 billion more that year if the companies had paid them a reasonable yield on their policies, which the commission estimated would have been 4 percent.

The report said that most persons who bought non-participating cash value whole life policies—that is, policies that don't pay dividends—in the 1950's and 1960's would do well to cash them in now and either buy term insurance of new dividend-paying whole life policies with much better yields.

The big emphasis in the report, however, was on a demand for much stricter disclosure in advance of the true cost of policies and the true yields and dividends over various periods of time on the different types of policies.

Chairman Michael Pertshuk of the FTC made perhaps the most damning comment. Pertshuk said, "No other product in our economy that is purchased by so many people for so much money is bought with so little understanding of its actual or comparative value."

The reaction to the FTC staff report, from both the public, and the life insurance industry, was explosive. All over the country people reading about it in the press or hearing about it on radio or television began calling or writing their insurance agents and brusquely ordering them to cash in whole life policies they had been paying on for years and write cheap term insurance instead.

A number of small insurance companies and independent agents began advertising term insurance or new comparatively high-yield, dividend-paying whole life policies to replace old policies. This created a lot of turmoil.

There are laws and formalities that must be observed by agents in changing an insured person's life policies. (See chapter 11).

Of course, the establishment companies and their trade associations denounced the FTC staff report. They said that it prejudged the issues, manipulated statistics, buried legitimate information favorable to older whole life cash value insurance, and confused the public, and that, generally speaking, the PTC staff showed a totally unjustifiable bias in favor of term insurance against whole life insurance.

A publication of the American Society of Chartered Life Underwriters called the staff report "an inexcusable and apparently deliberate effort to destroy public confidence in the life insurance business."

President Blake Newton of the American Council of Life Insurance (successor to the old Institute of Life Insurance) and the council's chairman, Armand C. Stalnaker, who was also chairman of General American Life Insurance Company, made numerous speeches and gave interviews denouncing the FTC staff report.

More significantly, in November 1979, the life companies succeeded in getting the Senate Commerce Committee to approve the Cannon Insurance Amendment to the Federal Trade Commission Act. Reporting on this vote, the December 1979 issue of the *Bulletin of the Life Underwriters Association of the City of New York* said that the Cannon Amendment "would make it clear that the FTC does not have the authority under the McCarran-Ferguson Act to investigate the business of life insurance."

The McCarran-Ferguson Act, passed in 1945, reaffirmed the life insurance companies' exemption from the federal antitrust laws, on the ground that the companies are adequately regulated by the states.

The significance of this vote is put in focus by the following editorial published by the *New York Times* on July 27, 1979, before the committee acted.

THE WHOLE TRUTH ABOUT LIFE INSURANCE

Would you put your money in a savings account paying 1.3 percent interest? According to a new Federal Trade Commission report, that's just about what many Americans do in purchasing life insurance. Life insurance companies hold more than $140 billion of the public's savings— roughly the amount held in passbook savings and loan association accounts—and generally pay returns far below the rate available in equally secure investments. The only plausible explanation is that policyholders don't realize how raw a deal they are getting. By the Commission's reckoning and ours, the most sensible solution is tough disclosure rules for life insurance companies.

The problem concerns "whole" life insurance. That is the most popular form involving savings as well as insurance. In 1977 about half of every insurance dollar was used to pay for death benefits and company expenses. The rest was socked away in insurance company investments on behalf of the policyholders or returned to them as dividends.

The holders of some of the policies examined by the Federal Trade Commission were paid a return, on the investment portion of other premiums, that was comparable to what they could have earned in the bank. But most policies, particularly those first written in the 1950's and early 1960's, paid far less. And virtually every purchaser of whole life insurance who allowed the policy to lapse within five years earned no interest at all.

Buyers can, of course, avoid the problem by avoiding whole life insurance and putting their savings in a bank. However, if people insist on buying whole life insurance—

and more important, if agents insist on selling it—then it is only reasonable that they be required to disclose the true rates of interest. That would permit comparison shopping, or at least give buyers some idea of what they are buying.

In 1976, the National Association of Insurance Commissioners—the organization of state regulators— prepared a model disclosure code; but it is inadequate, providing no means to compare the interest return on individual policies or the return on whole life with other investments. The Federal Trade Commission thus argues for major changes.

The FTC's whole life recommendations carry no legal weight; the McCarran-Ferguson Act delegates all insurance regulation to the states. But Americans spent $34 billion on life insurance in 1977. The market is so large and the inequities are so great that cost disclosure is imperative. If the states won't protect the consumer, there will be a strong case for Congress to do it for them.

However, President Carter endorsed the FTC staff report disclosure recommendations in a letter circulated to the governors of all the states early in 1980, on the eve of the Senate debate on the Cannon Insurance amendment to the Federal Trade Commission Act. The amendment was designed to keep the FTC's hands out of the insurance business.

The president wrote, "The (FTC) model regulation is designed to provide meaningful disclosure of life insurance costs . . . This is an important initiative the states can take to promote price competition and assure that the life insurance market is responsive to the needs of consumers.

The *Journal of Commerce* in New York called the president's letter to the governors "an end run around the Senate Commerce Committee's effort to tie the FTC's hands."

The life companies, meanwhile, began lining up

support of property and casualty insurers in support of their drive to curb the FTC and prevent a tough federally inspired disclosure program. They met with some success. Andre Maisonpierre, a vice president of the Alliance of American Insurers, a property-casualty trade association, backed the life companies' position.

Even before the FTC staff began the study that led to the bombshell report in mid-1979, there was increasing clamor for federal oversight of state regulation and even for repeal of the McCarran-Ferguson Act and for turning the regulation of the industry over to Washington.

These demands came up, somewhat obliquely, in 1973 and 1974, during hearings on the stifling of information about the life companies' financial practices and treatment of policyholders, before the Senate Subcommittee on Antitrust and Monopoly, headed by Senator Philip A. Hart.

Ralph Nader, the kingpin of consumerist crusaders, Herbert Denenberg, the former Pennsylvania Insurance Commissioner, Professor Joseph M. Belth, of Indiana University, a gadfly to the life insurance companies for many years, and many other critics testified. What he learned from the hearings led Senator Hart to introduce the Truth in Life Insurance Bill drafted by Dean Sharp, the subcommittee counselor. But after the untimely death of Senator Hart this bill languished. The committee is now headed by Senator Howard Metzenbaum, who has shown considerable investigative and crusading zeal, most recently in investigating abuses of credit life insurance.

But is disclosure enough, or will a federal standard result in the same kind of fiasco that efforts to achieve adequate and effective state disclosure standards have been, according to the *New York Times* editorial?

I think that the FTC staff report is on target in most of its criticisms of the insurance companies that dominate the industry, and I doubt seriously whether disclosure will be enough to bring on real and just reform. At least, it will not be enough for the federal government to require disclosure of the true costs and true yields of the different kinds of policies. Such a disclosure rule could not work miracles, simply because the business is too complicated and too filled with opportunities for greed.

It is also necessary to open completely the books and records of the mutual life insurance companies. These giants are run by self-perpetuating managements. Opening the windows and making their books freely available would disclose many things that might make the 1979 FTC staff report pretty tame reading by comparison. We would learn the details of much gross waste, poor management, and extravagant salaries and bonuses. In many cases, irregular and outright illegal activities and plain examples of corporate crime would be uncovered.

In May 1980, the FTC suffered a defeat in its efforts to bring about insurance industry reform when Senate and House conferees put severe limits on its continuing ability to conduct investigations of the industry. The commission can conduct new inquiries only if requested to do so by a majority vote of either the House or Senate Commerce Committees, and such authorization will expire at the end of the Congress in which it is given. The conferees also reaffirmed that the McCarran-Ferguson Act is the basis of national insurance policy and said that if the FTC wants the McCarran-Ferguson Act changed, it should ask Congress to change it instead of trying to bring about change by investigations of its own.

It would be too much to say that any groundswell for

repeal of the McCarran-Ferguson Act yet is evident, but more and more independent insurance agents and more academic economists are asking why the life insurance companies, since they do sell their products as investments, should not be under the same antitrust regulations as everyone else.

Probably the most unfortunate thing about the FTC staff report is its length. It is so cumbersome that the general press and broadcasters may not, to this day, have presented completely accurate digests of it.

David C. Fix, an FTC lawyer, stood up like Daniel in the lions' den before a meeting of the National Association of Life Underwriters in Detroit late in 1979 and implied that the press was responsible for the widespread impression that the FTC staff was hopelessly biased in favor of term insurance and against whole life insurance and was in fact prejudiced against the industry. But although he said that the FTC staff people were completely objective and interested only in making the observable facts public, Fix did not back down on any of the recommendations of the report.

What are the main things the FTC report urged, aside from publishing its own comparative estimates of the costs of different life insurance policies and the yields consumers can hope to realize from them? The best highlights of the report have appeared in the insurance trade press. In this day of expensive newsprint, the FTC report had little chance of competing for big space in the press or for time on the air with such stirring things as the aftermath of the Three Mile Island accident and events in Iran.

One of the important recommendations was that agents be required to furnish applicants for life insurance or annuities complete projections of the interest and dividend yields and calculations of the net cost of the life of the policy *before* the prospective buyer signs the application or gives the agent a check. By contrast, the model disclosure code of the National Association of Insurance Commissioners requires these disclosures to be made only when the policy is delivered.

Another recommendation of the report would give the policy buyer ten days in which to change his or her mind, return the policy, and demand a refund. Another would require agents in those states whose insurance departments issue consumers' guides to buying life insurance to furnish every prospective policy buyer with a copy of the guide.

But the controversial and the most complex of the recommendations concerned the type of indices to be used in helping consumers compare the relative merits of different policies in the same company and the policies offered by different companies.

The FTC staff wanted a single index figure used. It reports some companies now give prospective buyers as many as six different indices and that the so-called yardsticks are confusing and often contradictory. But it appeared that the FTC staff had little real hope of finding a satisfactory single index. Therefore, it urged the use of the Linton yield index, invented by actuary Albert M. Linton, which the FTC people like very much. as a companion to the surrender-unit-cost measurement favored by the National Association of Insurance Commissioners. The Linton yield index shows the annual rate of return on the cash value portion of a whole life insurance policy. A policy with a ten-year Linton yield index of 3.5 will earn 3.5 percent compound interest yearly on the savings portion of the policy if premiums are paid for ten years. The higher the Linton yield, the more attractive the policy.

But the Linton index doesn't measure many factors about a whole life insurance policy and the company that writes it. Neither does the surrender cost, for that matter. Nevertheless, some insurance companies are starting to quote Linton yields on their policies, and some of the consumer magazines are starting to use them in articles about the cost of insurance.

The surrender-unit cost is expressed as the dollar cost per thousand dollars of life insurance in force, based on cash surrender at varying periods. The lower the surrender-unit cost, the more attractive the policy is considered to be. But critics of this measurement say that it is even more meaningless by itself than the Linton yield index. It is used by *Consumer Reports* magazine.

The FTC staff report had some other conclusions that drew almost apoplectic reactions from life insurance bigshots. It said the non-participating cash value whole life policies of stock life companies were "low yield fixed value saving mediums uniquely unsuited to coping with accelerated inflation."

It pointed out that neither dividend-paying nor non-participating cash value whole life policies earn a penny for their purchasers in their early years. Both have big negative cash values in these years to pay the big selling costs, including hefty agents' commissions. And over the first twenty years of both kinds of policies. the FTC said. the yields were "extraordinarily low." At twenty years, the average yield for the dividend-paying policies was 3.71 percent and that for non-participating policies 2.4 percent. Compared with what a savings bank or some financial institution will pay you on your money these days, that's worse than peanuts. There are even insurance companies issuing tax-deferred annuities at interest rates much higher than cash value insurance results are these days.

However, the establishment life companies and their trade associations of agents rushed into the fray to say that the FTC people were just plain lying, that the average yield on whole life cash value policies was nearer 5.5 percent than 1.3 percent. They accused the FTC staff people of ignoring the value of the policies' fringe benefits and making unfair investment analyses similar to comparing apples with oranges. They also accused the FTC people of underestimating legitimate life insurance company expenses.

The report found some utterly astonishing variations in the yields on the same type of policy issued by different companies. It found one company paying only 1.52 percent on a $25,000 policy issued to a 35-year-old person while another company was paying 7.61 percent on an almost identical policy. Yet this information. which the FTC managed to uncover, is not available to the public and presumably not freely available to agents—so how are you going to go out and buy the policy that pays 7.61 percent? The implication is that it's some sort of "sweetheart deal."

In one of his speeches attacking the FTC staff report, Armand Stalnaker, the chairman of the Council of Life Insurance, said that he also believed the report to be a challenge and an opportunity to the industry "to reexamine our business." To that I say, "Amen!"

He went on to say that, from now on, life insurance cannot be a strictly commercial business but must become a quasi-public institution. Accordingly, he said, the companies "must perform their functions on a high plane, certainly on a plane that is substantially above what is expected generally in the marketplace."

He also warned that future criticism of the industry "will not be as clumsy or as ill-informed as that of the FTC staff report." I hope you find that his book fits that prophecy.

Let's look a minute at the implications of Stalnaker's remarks. What exactly is a quasi-public institution? A stockholder-owned electric utility comes instantly to mind. Does Stalnaker want life insurance companies to be regulated the way electric utilities are? The states rigorously set the return on investment an electric utility is permitted to earn, and if it earns more than that by miscalculation, it is required to make refunds to its customers.

Electric utilities cannot raise or lower rates a penny without the consent of the regulators. Their accounting procedures are rigorously prescribed by the regulators. Their salaries and expense budgeting are subject to regulatory control. The state regulators can disallow expenditures they deem excessive in setting the company's rate base on which its charges to consumers are set. In the last few years, as inflation has so cruelly eroded everyone's paycheck, the utilities and management consultants and executive recruiters who serve utility companies have been complaining that the states don't allow them a sufficient profit margin to pay competitive executive salaries. Therefore, they say, they are able to recruit only mediocre talent, and this leads to relatively inefficient management. This propaganda is somewhat overdone; most utilities are fairly well managed.

But the fact that Mr. Stalnaker is reduced to thinking

of life insurance companies as "quasi-public institutions" is most revealing.

Nineteen eighty-nine finds the life insurance industry, as a whole, on the defensive, with consumerism taking over and public opinion and "people power" pressing Congress to make changes that are all too necessary. Revocation of the McCarran-Ferguson Act, federal regulation, taking the handcuffs off the FTC, a "truth in life insurance selling" bill, and a self-regulatory body for insurance agents and financial planners are all in the discussion stages, along with federal regulation of the insurance industry.

The years that follow will be interesting indeed.

3. *Failures of State Regulation*

The apathy of most state regulatory officials. We don't have a Charles Evans Hughes now . . . The power of insurance lobbies in state capitals . . . The difficulty in getting outstanding insurance commissioners . . . State officials don't live up to the recommendations of their own professional association.

STATE REGULATION of life insurance as we know it today is largely the creation of two popular heroes of American political history.

One was a scholarly, determined, energetic man, an easterner of great personal charm and high intellect who went to bed on a November night in 1916 thinking he had been elected president of the United States, only to find out at breakfast that in the waning hours of the night California had swung the election, to keep Woodrow Wilson in the White House.

The other was a swashbuckling western rancher and mining lawyer, a rugged individualist who was loved by thousands but so authoritarian in many of his ideas that he was called a fascist. He was a frank imperialist and a military jingoist whose influence on Dwight Eisenhower and John Foster Dulles played no small part in ultimately getting us bogged down in the misguided and ill-fated war in Vietnam.

The first hero, of course, was Charles Evans Hughes. As a crusading young lawyer-politician, he conducted the famous investigation of the life-insurance companies by the New York legislature early in this century. State regulation already had failed the public dismally once. It was so benign and inept that companies went broke regularly, often fraudulently, and failed to pay death claims. Policies were frequently so deceitfully written that vaudeville comics made them a constant target of their acid wit. They cracked such jokes as the one about the widow who learned that the only way she could have collected insurance on her husband was if he had been killed by a falling star exactly at high noon on the twenty-ninth day of February.

Miraculously, Hughes cleaned up the whole mess in a single year. He got the New York legislature to adopt new laws and set up a model life-insurance regulatory system that was copied swiftly by all the other states. It ended all the worst abuses that were perceived at the time. It made Hughes a famous man, and even though he missed the White House he became chief justice of the United States Supreme Court and was universally admired.

But the regulatory system Hughes created didn't have to cope with serious inflation until long after World War II. It did have to cope with the Great Depression though, and it failed the test. Between the stock market crash in October 1929 and President Franklin Roosevelt's inauguration in 1933, so many businesses failed and so many people lost their jobs that the life-insurance companies were flooded with demands for policy loans and with requests from people wanting to cash in their cash value policies. The companies panicked.

Just before FDR's inauguration a secret meeting of executives of the big eastern establishment life companies and a score of state insurance commissioners was held in New York. At this meeting the companies tossed a bombshell on the floor: They proposed a moratorium on issuing policy loans and on honoring cash-value-surrender demands.

Since the companies and their agents had sold the policies largely by proclaiming that insured persons had an absolute right to borrow on their policies or cash them in, these state commissioners at first said that the moratorium proposal was grossly immoral and clearly illegal.

But these days before FDR took office, after the final collapse of the Hoover administration's economic policies had caused a total shutdown of the banks, the state insurance commissioners caved in, and the moratorium went into effect.

State regulation had failed the people a second time. The house that Hughes built had fallen down.

Starting in 1941, with the creation of the New York State Guarantors Corporation, steps were taken to prevent another such catastrophe. This guarantors corporation was so structured that if any life-insurance company domiciled in New York got in financial difficulty, all the other companies in the state would have to cooperate to rescue it. Many other states now have created such protective devices for their policyholders.

By the end of World War II some people were becoming concerned about another aspect of life-insurance regulation. The business had become increasingly concentrated in the big mutual firms and the larger multi-line stock companies that operated all over the country, or at least in many states. Clearly, these companies were engaged in interstate commerce, both in selling insurance and in their vast investment activity in securities and real estate. So a movement developed aimed at bringing them under federal regulation like the railroads, airlines, trucking lines, and the interstate securities-trading-and-investment industry.

The establishment companies did not like this idea. They had found it fairly easy to handle the state insurance departments by following the timehonored strategy of divide and conquer, but unified federal regulation would be a much more formidable police giant. Moreover, the White House could certainly be depended on to take a strong consumerist stand about life insurance if it was brought under federal regulation, and issues arising from it could be debated in national election campaigns.

Therefore, toward the end of the war, the companies put up a tremendous lobbying effort to preserve state regulations. They found an able champion and hero in Senator Pat McCarran of Nevada.

McCarran was the kind of man most people liked even if they hated his principles and denounced him roundly in public. He got the McCarran-Ferguson Act passed. Its guts are contained in a single short sentence: "No act of Congress shall be construed to invalidate, impair or supersede any law enacted by any state for the purpose of regulating insurance." This applies so long as the states do it effectively.

This means, of course, that any act of Congress to establish even a minor regulation or reform of the insurance business must first repeal the McCarran-Ferguson Act or else leave the real business of enforcement up to the states. All this was discussed at great length during the debate over whether Congress should set minimum standards for the states and no-fault automobile insurance.

The McCarran-Ferguson Act has also been an effective barrier against the maintaining of class-action lawsuits that policyholders have brought against life-insurance companies in the federal courts. Such a suit filed against four big mutual companies in 1972, alleging price-fixing, dubious accounting, cozy executive benefits, squandering of money on noninsurance ventures, and undemocratic self-perpetuation of management by failing to give the policyholders real voting power, was dismissed by a federal judge on the ground that the McCarran-Ferguson Act deprived the federal courts of jurisdiction.

Vociferous critics of state regulation—and their numbers are growing—insist that although many of the state commissioners are undeniably well meaning and capable, they are as a group rather easily manipulated and intimidated by the life-insurance establishment. The publicized activities of the National Association of Insurance Commissioners do little to contradict this charge. Most of the NAIC's programs are timid and unimaginative. So are the activities of the Conference of Insurance Legislators, which purports to be a band of knights in shining armor, members of legislatures dedicated to defending the rights of policyholders. The conference actually seems to act much more like a transmission belt or a front organization for the industry establishment.

A few years back, the NAIC put out a model state consumers' shopping guide to life insurance. It contains a vast amount of useful information, but critics claim it is biased in favor of whole-life cash-value insurance, as against term life, and seeks to gloss over some of the worst failings of life insurance.

One more big failure on the part of state insurance commissioners to put the interests of policyholders ahead of the privileges of the companies could bring on federal regulation and cause virtually all the state officials to be superseded and lose their jobs.

Two glaring failures of state regulation will become apparent when I discuss double dipping in credit life insurance (chapter 6) and scare selling in cancer insurance (chapter 5). Only three states have banned cancer insurance, and none of the state regulators has done anything to stop the enormous ripoff of the public by both insurance companies and banks and finance companies through overcharges on credit life insurance.

Another big problem with state regulation is that it is impossible to insulate it sufficiently from politics. After all, most of the regulators are political appointees and must depend on members of the state legislatures for moral support and for the funds to operate their departments. All politicians and bureaucrats are vulnerable in some degree to pressures from people who have axes to grind and therefore make political contributions in order to influence legislative and departmental policy. The life-insurance business has long maintained powerful lobbies in all the state capitals for this purpose. Moreover, the state regulators are dependent to a considerable extent on the companies for technical and financial information on which to base their decisions.

On the other hand, their own self-esteem and concern for their status forbids the regulators to be servile toward the insurance companies. They must prevent outright defaults on policies and bankruptcy scandals and must assist in prosecutions of insurance people for embezzlement, fraudulent accounting, violations of the securities laws, and other criminal acts.

It boils down to the fact that state regulation costs the taxpayers a tidy sum, and there is an increasing feeling that the public does not get enough benefits from it.

The sixty-four-dollar question is, How can federal intervention improve this situation? Probably in two ways. The federal government is vastly bigger and more powerful than any state. People who scarcely know what city is the capital of their home state listen when a Washington bureaucrat speaks. People who won't go to the trouble to vote for governor do not fail to vote in presidential elections.

But the federal bureaucrat also is more vulnerable to public opinion than the state official. A federal agency is a shining target for the Ralph Naders and other crusaders, who would often be reduced to thumb-sucking despair if they could take their causes only to the fifty separate state legislatures and a multitude of offices filled with state bureaucrats.

4. *The Confession*

The gradual impact of the confidential 1974 Trend Report of the Institute of Life Insurance, which concluded that the business is on a "self destruct course." This document is a tacit confession that the life companies have long grossly overcharged their customers. It may be fifteen years old, but it is more true today than ever.

IN SPITE OF THEIR bitter criticism of the FTC staff report's conclusions, it is plain fact that the leaders of the life-insurance establishment admitted the truth of virtually all the report's charges five years before they were made.

This confession was not intentional, nor was it made available to the public or even to the army of life-insurance companies' employees and agents. Nevertheless, enough copies of this tacit confession were printed for private perusal by the industry's top executives so that eventually several thousand photocopies were made of the twenty-six page document, and many people learned of its contents. Undoubtedly the FTC staff obtained copies of it.

So did many, if not all, state insurance commissioners, although nothing happened to indicate that the 1974 *Trend Report* of the Institute of Life Insurance (called the American Council of Life Insurance since it moved from New York to Washington, which is a more convenient place for lobbying) made much impression on the state regulatory officials.

The institute had been in the habit of publishing periodic trend reports for some time, but the 1974 document was a real blockbuster. It was based on abstracts provided by more than a hundred top company executives, and it made the chilling declaration that the four industry leaders chosen to write the final draft had concluded that, in the present inflationary climate, the industry was "on a self-destruct course" if it continued its "present emphasis on individual whole life products."

The four persons who reached this conclusion were Kenneth M. Wright, chief economist of the American Life Insurance Associations; Mona G. Coogan, manager of business economics for the Metropolitan Life Insurance Company; J. Robert Ferrari, chief economist of the Prudential Insurance Company of American; and Francis H. Schott, vice-president and economist of the Equitable Life Assurance Society of the United States.

Like many confidential corporate forecasts intended for top executives, this 1974 life insurance *Trend Report* attempted to predict various future prospects based on alternative possibilities. The possibilities were labeled Scenarios 1, 2, and 3. Scenario 1—continued high inflation at rates exceeding ten percent a year—is what eventually happened, so that's the one we'll deal with mainly in this chapter.

Scenario 2 hoped for a leveling off of inflation to an

annual rate of 4.5 percent, with no new wars or such nasty events as the cutoff of Iranian oil has proved to be. Scenario 3 also envisioned a big drop in inflation, after a rise to about twelve percent by 1977, resulting in local wars around the world and a wave of strikes and other disturbances so large that it would be followed by an authoritarian reaction, a crackdown in the United States in 1978 that would be, according to one's personal interpretation, either a fascist coup (the *Trend Report* used no labels, however) or a healthy return to law and order and sensible economics coupled with a "vigorous fiscal policy"—a phrase that means high taxes for the masses and very low taxes for the wealthy and powerful.

The four who wrote the *Trend Report* obviously felt that Scenario 1 was what we were going to get, and they were dead right. Also, they found all three scenarios equally unpleasant. Under Scenario 3, for example, they didn't think a dictator or just a government committed to "centralization of economic management" would have much sympathy or time for the life-insurance business. They said such a regime likely "would largely destroy the opportunity of individuals to fund their own personalized security programs"—that is, the opportunity for life-insurance companies to sell cash-value policies or even such straight investment instruments as annuities.

In addition to the remark about being on a self-destruct course, the "general comments" starting on page 8 of the *Trend Report* were enough to make the average life-insurance agent's hair stand up straight and to make policyholders reach for the telephone to call their agents and cancel much of their insurance. So the report was kept carefully out of the hands of the public and the rank-and-file agents.

But one of the comments would have pleased a lot of agents. The report said that the first two scenarios "foretell such expansion of the indexed benefits of Social Security that the large middle market would be swallowed by government benefits." Even before the *Trend Report* a number of insurance agents had complained bitterly that Social Security is unfair competition with their business, particularly since Social Security is not really insurance— it is financed to a substantial degree out of general tax revenues, in addition to payroll deduction and employer contributions.

The other harsh forecasts in these general comments were:

1. "The means to pay premiums for individual [whole-life cash-value] contracts would disappear in tax expansion."
2. "The business might seek such options as floating or indexed rates for policy loans or even a release from the obligation of guaranteed cash values."
3. "The purchasing power of permanent life insurance will be impaired."
4. "Conditions suggest the likelihood of a major shift away from traditional cash value, whole life insurance with its fixed dollar saving element toward various forms of term insurance."
5. "Term insurance may have to be higher priced to provide the agent with compensation lost as the result of diminished whole life sales."
6. "The conditions would be good for a greater reliance on group term insurance and, particularly among the masses, on Social Security."
7. "There could be a massive drain on individual life

insurance reserves and the underlying investments."

8. "Mutual companies [and stock companies selling dividend paying policies] might review dividend policy. This could include a look at the investment year method, the possibility of a level rather than an increasing dividend flow, and possible reduction of terminal dividends to recognize the market value loss due to withdrawal of funds when asset values are depressed on a current yield basis."

Of course, the most immediately important of these conclusions is number four, which admits that people are finding that moderately priced term insurance providing adequate death benefits is far more valuable than costly whole-life cash-value policies, which often accomplish little except to earn fat commissions for agents and big profits for the life companies. It gives the lie to practically everything the companies have preached for more than a century.

If some of the forecasts of the *Trend Report* are realized, such as number two and number eight, the entire structure of the mammoth life-insurance industry will be changed forever. I predict that such moves would almost mean further encroachment on the part of government, through amendments to the Social Security law, that would make new sales of life insurance impossible.

The remark about using the investment-year method for calculating policy dividends actually means cheating older policyholders so more attractive dividends can be offered to new policy buyers. James F. Reiskytl, associate actuary of Northwestern Mutual Life Insurance Company, charged early in 1979, in a letter to the National Association of Insurance Commissioners, that the investment-year method of fixing dividends amounted to illegal manipulation of dividends in order "to beat out competition."

In using the investment-year method, the company calculates policy dividend-payment rates on present yields of investments instead of the cumulative average yields. Thus, they do not include interest on investments made some years back, at much lower interest rates. Therefore, in a period of higher rates, the dividends offered new policyholders can be made to look more attractive than they should, and this is done at the expense of existing policyholders.

Changing Times magazine said that one of the biggest mutual companies already has adopted the investment-year method of calculating dividends and that an official of the company could see nothing wrong with doing it that way.

Other important conclusions concerned what the 1974 *Trend Report* authors considered to be the outlook for new life-insurance products. After reiterating the view that term insurance would increasingly replace whole-life cash-value policies, they said group term life insurance would become increasingly important because "it is an indexed product to the extent that it is related to the employee's salary."

The report pointed out that there are numerous objections to indexing as a means of dealing with inflation (the most important objection is that it can lull people into thinking the inflation is being coped with), but added, "If our psychology is to be indexed then, of course, indexed life insurance must play an important role."

Like whole life, group life insurance also has its inequities, even though it is relatively cheap and most times is paid for entirely by the employer. A friend of mine who is still employed at his maximum salary had his group-life coverage cut in half three years ago because of his age. It doesn't seem fair.

The report also concluded that companies will sell a wider range of policies because "without a wide range of products it will be very difficult for an agent to survive financially." On this subject, the *Trend Report* indulged in a frankness the authors would hardly have liked to submit to public gaze. It said, "While this does not relate to the type of life insurance product likely to be sold, it does speak to the product mix the life insurance agent is likely to have in his portfolio. And, therefore, it speaks to the amount of time, training and expertise the agent may need for selling and servicing the life products of the future."

Sounds nice, but what does it really mean? The more you look at it, the more it seems as if life insurance is getting ready to substitute packaging and marketing for full measure and worth of products.* It reminds one of a film called *The Hucksters*, which starred Clark Gable, Deborah Kerr, and Sidney Greenstreet. Greenstreet played the president of the Beautee Soap Company, a role obviously patterned on the career of George Washington Hill, the advertising genius of American Tobacco Company. He tells Gable in the film, "There isn't any damn difference in soap except a little perfumery. All the rest is advertising and selling. We outadvertise and outsell our competitors; that's all there is to it."

After showing their distaste for policies indexed to cope with inflation, the *Trend Reports* authors next deal with proposals for automatic increases in coverage, but

---

*How right this is! The universal life scam. (See chapter 13.)

add, "We recognize that the agent frequently objects to automatic increases in coverage, but we wonder if that psychology can be permitted to predominate in the future."

The FTC staff report made crystal clear that many agents object to automatically increased coverage because it deprives them of the opportunity to write a new policy with a fat initial premium that they can now write when dear Doctor Rostomy's practice is doing so well that he decides he needs more life insurance. The inference of the *Trend Report* remark on automatic coverage also is crystal clear: If automatic coverage increases turn out well for the companies, the agents can swallow it or get lost.

I can only say that in this area, I disagree not only with the FTC staff report, but with the *Trend Report* as well. Instead of preventing agents from earning a rightful livelihood after creating present and future business for an insurance company, I would prefer that commissions be paid on automatic increases in coverage and the money be obtained by eliminating waste in the home offices of the companies.

As a matter of fact, some articles in the insurance trade press and the general press have recently suggested that the general agency system may have to be abandoned. And the *Trend Report* predicts considerable difficulty in recruiting young persons to go into the life-insurance business in the coming years because "inflation will abort thrift as an achievable goal in the minds of the public, and this will render undesirable a sales career in exclusively life sales."

This condition has existed for the forty-five years I have been around the industry, but it took till 1974 for others to wake up to this fact. If insurance people are doing a professional job, they must know and sell all lines of insurance and even other money products.

We can wonder whether young people being interviewed for life-insurance sales jobs are being told this.

The report also said that the cost of recruiting agents has skyrocketed and the industry's old problem of a high turnover of young salespeople is not getting any better. College employment offices will tell you quite bluntly that when the on-campus recruiting season comes each year, insurance companies are reduced to taking the leavings, the graduates whose average grades weren't high enough to win them good offers from companies in the fields for which they trained. So you find a lot of people with engineering and other professional degrees among young life-insurance salespersons. You also find a lot of people who trained to be teachers but couldn't find jobs in that overcrowded field.

The *Trend Report* also forecast the death of a lot of small and medium-sized life companies. That hardly surprises anyone who watches the stock market even casually. Very few life stocks have done very well since their prices peaked out in 1964–65.

The report also forecast a possible "detrimental effect on the persistency rate of our business." That's a fancy way of saying that more people will stop paying on their policies.

And a cutback was forecast in lavish and ostentatious offices for life-company executives. Drastic changes in employee compensation were predicted. The concluding pages dwelt heavily on one theme—that the industry would have to get rid of a lot of humble and marginal workers and make promotion faster for good employees. (One major company shocked its employees with top-to-bottom layoffs in 1978.)

Another admission in the report was that companies that are already selling wide portfolios of term insurance "appear to be in a better position to weather the inflationary storms" than the companies still concentrating on whole life.

That also seems to put the lie to a vast amount of the propaganda the establishment companies have preached as gospel for a hundred and twenty-five years.

But perhaps the most revealing statement in the whole study is at the bottom of page 22: "Top executives, not so mobile as the technical group, might suffer the most and, therefore, innovative bonus systems might be in order."

I have dwelled much on the *Trend Report* which is now fifteen years old. I must emphasize that much has come about during the past fifteen years that makes this report a reality and that many of the things to come in the life insurance industry will, in the end, be good for consumers all across America.

5. *Typical Abuses*

A typical life insurance story and high-pressure mail order selling . . . Conglomerate bottom-line perils . . . Scare selling: who needs cancer insurance? . . . TV ads.

MORE THAN A CENTURY AGO, Phineas T. Barnum remarked of suckers, "There's one born every minute."

However, the astute showman actually had an affectionate regard for suckers. He believed in giving them a pretty fair shake for their money. His circus, menagerie, concerts, and other attractions always were first rate, even though the ballyhoo by which he sold tickets and gained worldwide publicity was composed of elaborate and barefaced hokum. He also knew that the customers were amused by the ballyhoo.

There always have been people in the world, though, quite as aware as Barnum of the ever-renewable supply of suckers but totally lacking Barnum's conscience. They operate on the principle that the easiest and most profitable way to do business is to rip the suckers off mercilessly, not just by using deceitful advertising and ballyhoo to make sales, but by delivering a shoddy product, a product that is grossly overpriced or isn't really needed.

The life insurance business has had more than its share of these gross abuses. The endowment policy was one such abuse. We will see later that the heavily front-end-loaded annuity is another. Cancer insurance, a current fad, is also such an abuse.

Still another abuse is the mail-order sale of so-called budget-priced term insurance at prices that turn out to be at least twice those of other comparable policies. I am not attacking all mail-order marketers of life insurance. Doubtless, most mail-order policies are quite fairly priced, considering that frequently no medical examination is required to buy them. But some are quite plainly abuses. Unfortunately, some of the mail-order policies that are the poorest values are offered by life insurance subsidiaries of conglomerates.

Many insurance companies—life, property and casualty, and even multi-line enterprises—have been acquired in recent years by industrial and commercial conglomerates. Some conglomerates have even established new insurance companies to take advantage of special opportunities related to their other enterprises; these include health insurance, credit life insurance, or automobile-maintenance insurance extending coverage some years beyond the manufacturers' warranties.

These invasions of the insurance field by noninsurance corporations have raised questions. In the frenzied merger activity in the United States in the past twenty years, the business world has seen plenty of prosperous businesses destroyed by mergers, either by looting, cynical liquidation to reduce competition or by the inability of the acquiring company to give the purchased business as good management as it enjoyed under its original owners. That could happen to some insurance companies gobbled up by conglomerates.

A lot of these unfortunate occurrences are the direct consequence of the "bottom line" management philosophy so religiously taught in our graduate business schools. Candidates for the degree of master of business administration are taught that their careers will depend on how regularly they can show an increase for the departments or subsidiaries they are given to run on the "bottom line"—yield on invested capital or as a percentage of sales, according to the nature of the business. This can lead to cynical management abuses.

It is this "bottom line economics" that is part of what is making so much of American business operate on the rip-off principle, and it is probably responsible in no small degree for the decline in our national productivity and our failing competitive position in international markets. The aim of this philosophy is to get an ever-bigger yield out of every dollar of sales any way you can, and never mind the consumers. The thinking is, "They are born suckers, and if we don't take them somebody else will."

Naturally, runaway inflation increases business cynicism and makes businessmen justify in their own eyes this kind of rapacious marketing.

But it gyps the people who buy the policies horribly. The insurance is sold by following Joseph Goebbels's famous maxim that the bigger the lie is and the more often and the more loudly it is repeated, the easier it is to get people to believe it—and buy.

A young couple in their twenties or thirties does not

need a paltry ten thousand or even twenty thousand dollars in death protection today. They need one hundred thousand to one million, according to what they can afford.

The big trouble, as we have pointed out earlier, is that life insurance pricing is downright chaotic. However, if it were only the complex age tables and the equally complex tables on face amounts and special benefits, then any reasonably well educated agent with a hand calculator could figure out the answers to the really important questions quickly.

But the agent will flounder on company-to-company comparisons, with their baffling and often totally illogical contradictions. Only the very experienced agent can find his or her way through this jungle with reasonable promptness. The agent, of course, is forbidden even to make the effort. The establishment life insurance companies have created a climate in which people literally have no idea what the price of insurance ought to be. The companies have fostered this public ignorance and exploited it for generations to make high profits.

The managements of some of the conglomerates that have pushed into the life insurance business undoubtedly see in this widespread public ignorance a golden opportunity to make big killings. In what other line of business are the customers so ill-informed about the product's actual worth, so like sheep ready for the shearing?

Everyone knows how to compare the values of things sold in stores; and although you can sell a really fancy automobile for a big price on glamour, no one's going to pay Cadillac prices for compact cars. But that's precisely what some of the "bottom line" insurance company managers are selling—and they're getting away with it.

From time to time, though, a life insurance fad comes along with its sales appeal based largely on scare selling—arousing unjustified fear among prospective customers and using that fear to reap high profits while providing inferior insurance benefits. We are being subjected to such a fad now—it's called cancer insurance.

Cancer insurance is not exactly a gigantic deal. The total amount of premium income it brings in probably is small.

Not many life companies write cancer insurance. At least three states have outlawed the business, and half a dozen others have cracked down hard on the advertising and sales techniques of the companies that do sell it.

Changing Times magazine denounced cancer insurance as "a bad buy" in its December 1979 issue. In Congress, the House Select Committee on Aging has been investigating the business. The federal General Accounting Office reported that the loss ratio of the companies that sell it—that is, the proportion of premium income that they actually paid out in claims—ranged downward from fifty-five percent to an astounding nineteen percent for one company. Even fifty-five percent is a very low loss ratio for any life insurance or health insurance operation. By contrast Blue Cross-Blue Shield is a nonprofit operation. Nevertheless, it makes enough money to pay very good salaries on that high loss ratio.

The handful of companies that sell cancer insurance are big advertisers, using direct mail, periodicals, and radio and television to carry their sales messages. At least three of the companies have been accused by public officials or agencies of deceptive advertising and unfair sales practices.

The main complaints against the companies selling

cancer insurance are:

• In spite of the big face values of the policies, many of them do not pay any more for cancer treatment and care than conventional medical and hospitalization policies or Medicare pay for the same premium dollar.

• Massachusetts investigators said cancer insurance sold in the state paid for only about thirty percent of the cost of a typical serious cancer case.

• The Federal Trade Commission staff said a cancer insurance policy is like a lottery ticket "and not a very good gamble either."

• *Changing Times* said many cancer insurance policies have major exclusion clauses denying benefits to the insured that are not readily apparent to the policy buyer and are not adequately explained.

• The policies pay only for "definitive cancer treatment" as a rule; they pay nothing for diagnosis, pathology reports, or cancer-related complications.

• Some of the policies pay for chemotherapy or radiological treatment only if the patient is hospitalized; yet current medical practice is to give most of these treatments on an outpatient basis. The policies usually pay nothing for rehabilitation, which also is done on an outpatient basis.

• The policies do not take effect until 60 to 120 days after purchase. If a malignancy is discovered during this period it may not be covered by the cancer policy.

• As stated earlier in this chapter, the companies exaggerate the prevalence of cancer in the United States grossly in their advertising, exploiting and even creating a hysterical fear of cancer.

• The companies spread the idea that a person can

collect simultaneously under two or more health insurance policies, including a cancer policy, although this by no means is always true.

Although cancer insurance appears to resemble renewable-term life insurance and is sold without a medical examination, and although the premiums are relatively modest, remember that it pays no death benefit unless death is caused directly by cancer and no disability benefits except for cancer.

So the cancer insurance business would appear to be another example of insurance huckstering, abusing the basic concept of life insurance to rip off the public by selling people protection they don't really need.

As a matter of fact, a close analysis shows that the perils that any individual faces in life are so numerous that to insure against each of these hazards would necessitate forking over your whole salary check each week to insurance companies.

In this discussion of abuses by the insurance industry, I can't let the opportunity go by to mention one of the latest abuses and, to me, one of the most offensive. I'm talking about the latest trend in insurance advertising. I'm sure you've seen those commercials, which are increasingly present on our TV screens, that feature prominent personalities pushing life or health insurance, usually for older people. These advertisements play on the consumer's trust of a familiar, well-like entertainment figure and hope that, subliminally, that trust will convert to trust in the product they are selling.

A big mistake! These personalities, regardless of how popular with the public they are for their acting or entertainment abilities, are not insurance experts. In fact, many probably know next to nothing about insurance. While I question the credibility of a performer who would "push" a product about which he is ill-informed, I put the greatest share of blame on the insurance companies, who are propagating yet another form of minor fraud on the television-viewing consumer. So little information is given about these products that no one could possibly judge their value from a brief thirty-second commercial, and no amount of famous faces can make up for an insurance product that is a poor value.

We can't help seeing these commercials, but we can be aware that they are nothing more than paid advertisements, flashy ways to promote sales by paying respected actors and performers large amounts of money to seemingly "endorse" their products.

The products sold through this kind of advertising are virtually worthless. They do take advantage of the gullible consumer and the concerned senior citizen. I wish they could be outlawed throughout the U.S.

I'll talk later in this book about the increasingly terrible public image of the life insurance industry. But for now, let me say to those in the establishment industry who worry that the public doesn't have respect for their profession, is it any wonder? Given just the abuses we've touched upon in this chapter, how can it be surprising that consumers rate the insurance industry as one of the nation's least-respected?

6. Double Dipping in Credit Life

One-third of the annual premium collections on credit life insurance probably represents overcharges, and to add insult to injury, the borrowing consumer has to pay high interest on the premium. A fight looms in Congress to end this abuse.

ANOTHER LIFE INSURANCE scandal that is cheating Americans of huge sums is the gross abuse of credit life insurance.

About $242.98 billion worth of credit life insurance was in force in the United States at the end of 1987. The 1988 *Life Insurance Fact Book* says that $2.1 billion was collected in 1987 in credit life premiums, but actual collections were undoubtedly much higher, because premiums are collected in advance for loans running for eighteen months to several years, but the companies report only the portions applicable to the current year. There seems to be good reason to suspect that at least one-third of the collections represents scandalous overcharges.

Unlike the abuses of whole life cash value insurance, credit life chicanery is an abuse of term insurance, selling the coverage at inflated rates of from four to ten times the cost of other term life insurance. Indeed short-term credit life rates appear to be much higher than those of either whole life cash value insurance or health insurance. The excuse generally given for the high rates is that no medical examination is required and no questions are asked the insured about her or his health. But this is not entirely true. Credit life insurance is always written to guarantee payment of a loan in case of the death of the borrower, and many lending institutions ask questions about the borrower's health before making the loan. The mere fact that the loan application has been accepted is thus a guarantee to the insurance company that the borrower is reasonably healthy.

Credit life insurance is cynically claimed by its vendors to be cheap—"only a few pennies a day"—to relieve your survivors of the painful necessity of paying off the loan if you die. Don't you believe it! Credit life insurance can add hundreds of dollars to the cost of even a moderately-priced automobile financed for five years.

The particularly loathsome aspect of credit life insurance is a "double-dipping rip-off" of the insured borrowers by two sets of deceptive hucksters, the insurance companies and the banks and finance companies who serve as their vendors and who get the bigger share of the rip-off profits. They accomplish this because the premium is not paid directly by the insured, who is the borrower, but is added to the face amount of the loan and interest is charged on it at the same rate as the principal of the loan.

That's only the tip of the iceberg. What the gullible borrower who consents to having his or her loan insured by credit life insurance (it is not required by law, no matter what the bank or finance company officer may tell you) doesn't know is that banks and finance companies often deliberately purchase the most expensive credit life insurance they can find and pass the cost on to borrowers because that inflates their commissions as vendors of the insurance and gives them bigger premiums to charge interest on.

Even though it is not required by law, the lending company can require a credit life insurance policy covering the loan of its own volition. But if the lender tells you it's required by law, you can sue for damages. The reason for the deception is usually to stop the loan applicant from shopping around to find cheaper insurance. There have been so many complaints recently about the abuses of credit life insurance that the Consumers Credit Life Insurance Association, composed of insurance companies that sell the stuff, told the Illinois State Insurance Department it now favors giving borrowers more options about whether they will buy the coverage at all and even a grace period to cancel it if they change their minds.

This chastened attitude undoubtedly stems from a wave of reports that lending institutions had failed to tell borrowers the amount their loans had been increased to pay for credit life insurance or to give them any information about the cost of the insurance. That is clearly illegal but the practice appears to be widespread. In December 1979, Senator Howard Metzenbaum asked the Justice

Department to investigate for possible criminal prosecution a case in which Beneficial Finance Company failed for twelve years to inform a blind couple living in Philadelphia that they were being charged for credit life insurance on their loans. A company official then told the couple that the insurance was required, which Senator Metzenbaum said was not the case. And in a lawsuit the couple accused Beneficial of adding to their loan contract a false statement that they had consented to the purchase of the insurance. According to *The Insurance Advocate* for December 1, 1979, to forestall further legal action, Beneficial canceled the blind couple's $1,200 loan balance and paid them $2,000 cash, plus $1,750 in legal fees.

Senator Metzenbaum planned late in 1979 to introduce a bill to set minimum federal standards for the states in regulating credit life insurance. He said that the Senate Judiciary Antitrust Subcommittee had been investigating credit life insurance for twelve years, and during that time the state regulatory authorities had done almost nothing to curb the abuses.

With a few noteworthy exceptions, he said, the state officials are not protecting consumers from systematic overcharges and other abuses by credit life insurance companies. He said that, for most consumers, credit life insurance costs two to four times as much as other term insurance and sometimes much more than that.

J. Robert Hunter, deputy administrator of the Federal Insurance Administration, was quoted by Brendan Jones in the *New York Times*, May 19, 1979, as saying that credit life insurance costs up to ten times as much as other life insurance or health insurance. Hunter told Jones that all credit life insurance "is a rip-off, most people don't need the stuff."

Senator Metzenbaum said that In many states less than one third of the premiums collected on credit life insurance go to pay claims, thus giving the insurance companies—and the banks and finance companies acting as their vendors—an enormous melon to split up. It is a seller's market for the creditors—that is, for the banks and finance companies—and the senator and Hunter both said that the bizarre "reverse competition" makes it a bonanza. Metzenbaum said that this phenomenon alone demonstrates the need for effective price regulation in credit life insurance and that if the states continue their apathetic attitude, Congress will have to do something about it.

Every state except Alaska has set a ceiling on credit life insurance rates but Metzenbaum and other critics say that these ceilings are too high. Metzenbaum said that in forty states the ceilings are so high that they permit minimum loss ratios of less than fifty percent of premiums collected. He said they ought to be lowered until the companies are required to pay out on claims about eighty percent of what they collect in premiums. The National Association of Insurance Commissioners seems to be veering in favor of aiming at minimum loss ratios of sixty percent and a general ceiling on rates of fifty cents per hundred dollars of insured loan. At least three major credit life underwriters testified to that effect before Metzenbaum's committee in November 1979.

Metzenbaum said that rates based on a minimum loss ratio of fifty percent are probably costing Americans nine hundred million dollars a year more to insure their consumer loans against death than if the companies had to assume that they would pay out eighty percent of their premium collections in loss claims.

The senator also said that there is much coercive selling in credit life insurance—a strong implication that if you don't go along with the lending company's deal and buy its credit insurance, you may not get the loan.

It was also testified that the actual national average annual rate on credit life insurance was around 65.5 cents per hundred dollars of loan insured and that adoption of the NAIC's sixty-percent loss limit could cut that to around 41.7 cents.

This testimony came from James H. Hunt, director of the Massachusetts State Rating Bureau. He said that in general, credit life insurance is costing people fifty-seven percent more than what the NAIC recommends, and he criticized his fellow state officials for not moving more vigorously to follow their own association's program.

New York has one of the lowest average rates on credit life insurance in the country, about 44 cents, but Irene Alpert of the New York State Insurance Department staff said that's still too high. She said the rate ought to be not more than 41 cents. She was quoted to this effect by Brendan Jones in the *New York Times.*

Jones said that the interest the banks charge on credit life insurance premiums they advance to borrowers is a bonanza at present rates and that if interest rates should fall sharply after the big 1979 rise, the banks would continue to collect the high 1979 interest rates on a very large volume of these premium advances for some time to come.

What can the individual do about the scandalous conditions in credit life insurance? Not as much as he or she can do about other life insurance abuses. The reason is that many credit life insurance transactions are small and not worth going to a lot of trouble and fuss over. The insurance companies and the lenders rely on public apathy and on the fact that the ordinary borrower is so pressed for time that she or he will submit to their deception and thievery.

But if it's a fairly hefty loan—financing a car or college tuition, for example—it will pay to take the time to exercise your rights. Remember these facts:

• Credit life insurance is not required by law, no matter what a bank or finance-company official may tell you.

• The lending institution can require you to take credit life insurance as a condition of granting the loan, but it cannot require you to buy the policy it is selling. You can shop around and buy your own, and by so doing you will at least save paying interest on the premium at today's high rates.

• You can and should demand a statement of the exact cost of the credit life insurance you are offered. If it is more than about forty-five cents per hundred dollars of loan per year, it is high. But nearly all the rates you are offered are certain to be quite excessive.

• Shopping for reasonably priced credit life insurance may not be easy, but your independent life insurance agent may be able to help you. He or she may be able to find coverage at a more reasonable cost.

• In New York, Pennsylvania, and probably many other states you should be able to get useful information about buying credit life insurance more reasonably by writing or telephoning your state department of insurance.

You might also write your senator and representative

in Congress and your state legislators demanding that something drastic be done to curb the credit life insurance rip-off. But why bother? Just keep away from credit life insurance. You don't need it, particularly if you have already purchased death insurance protection in large quantity to protect your family.

7. A Smug Industry

Insurance companies are not public spirited . . . They do little for policyholders hurt by inflation . . . They drag their feet on accident prevention, crime, educational advancement, and other social issues.

EARLY IN 1979, the American Council of Life Insurance held a conclave on inflation at Williamsburg, Virginia. Out of the meeting came a big, elaborately-printed publicity kit, replete with canned speeches and press releases, sent to all the life companies and many agency heads.

After perusing the kit, one might be pardoned for concluding that its only contribution to combating inflation was that the manuscript pages were typed on both sides of the paper. The pieces in the kit posed a lot of questions, all of which had been raised before by numerous economists, businessmen, educators, politicians, and journalists. The Council of Life Insurance turned out

73

to be more timid than these other Jeremiahs in saying what ought to be done about inflation.

Executives of insurance companies are generally known to be timid, and very few like to act responsibly for fear of rocking the boat. More important—are the life insurance companies really ready to help educate the multitudes to stem the tide of runaway inflation and save America?

The only area on which the canned speeches were very positive concerned the appalling impact of inflation on the cash value life insurance business—company profits and agents' commissions. The kit's silence was deafening (if reading matter can be deafening) on the really big question—what, if anything, the life companies are willing to do to help the millions of older and no-so-old policyholders who are stuck with high-priced life policies whose cash values and death benefits have been eroded in comparison with other, more conventional savings instruments. Are the companies willing to come clean and tell the policyholders the truth? Are they prepared to offer older customers something better at affordable premium prices in exchange for the depreciated policies?

The answer is—silence. When the companies say anything to these older customers they urge them in shrill tones to continue paying the sacrificial tribute to the privileged life insurance establishment. This attitude shows that in spite of their pious posture of being a great benefactor of humanity, the life insurance companies do not constitute a public-spirited business.

Except in medical research, where it could expect to reap a huge return in longer life expectancy and, hence, longer premium collections, life insurance has not been particularly generous in its contributions to the public welfare. Nor have the companies been bold and vigorous in taking actions and stands calculated to help society advance. Steel barons, automobile tycoons, department-store owners, oil millionaires, publishing magnates, and successful Wall Streeters seem to have been much more generous.

Herbert Denenberg, the former Pennsylvania insurance commissioner, says the life companies are apathetic about the public welfare. He said that his views about the life companies had mellowed a little in recent years because he had encountered so many more villainous attitudes toward consumers on the part of other industries. However, he still thinks the life companies are too content to sit on their hands. He said that they collect statistical information that reveals serious problems in society, but as a rule they don't follow through and try to get something done about the problems.

Denenberg was made to feel the political power of the life companies after he exposed their nefarious pricing practices while he was insurance commissioner. He resigned to run for the United States Senate, in the expectation that he could regain the commissionership if he didn't make it into the Senate, but the life companies succeeded in blocking his reappointment by exerting political pressure.

In his column in the *Philadelphia Daily News* on January 3, 1980, Denenberg said that it is surprising that the public buys as much life insurance as it does "when you consider the confusing and inept marketing methods of the industry. . . . The Public Enemy No. 1 of the life insurance industry is the life insurance industry itself."

Of course, in saying that the industry is not public spirited, I am referring to the companies. Many company general agents and many independent life insurance agents are public spirited. They work hard in charity drives, serve on the boards of many worthwhile activity groups, and often are generous with their own financial contributions. But the companies, sitting on over one billion worth of assets as of the end of 1987, obviously could do a great deal more than they have. Their ineffectual and almost totally self-serving approach to fighting inflation is typical.

What have they done about education? Offhand, I can't think of an American university or college that was founded by the benevolence of an insurance magnate, nor do I know of any large-scale scholarship programs or long-term research projects funded by life insurance companies except those few which are calculated to increase life insurance profits if they are successful. Even in these areas the life company funding is likely to be small compared with what comes from government agencies and other private and commercial sources.

We have in the United States a crisis in our school systems. It is caused only partly by money shortages. Population shifts, language barriers, racial tensions, the baleful influence on kids of commercial television, the fact that too many mothers have to hold down jobs and the children are left on their own much of the day, at least after school hours—all these are more serious matters than the money shortages. But money could help alleviate some of these problems, and a rich industry like the life insurance industry could do something. It could well afford to offer help in finding solutions. It shows no signs of doing so.

Most of my readers have learned of the terrible toll that our inferior school system has taken on the literacy level of our poor citizens during the past several decades. Why hasn't this industry, so rich and supposedly so humanitarian, done something to effect a better school system throughout the country?

Slaughter on the highways in one of the worst problems in America today. The property and casualty insurance industry, much of which is teamed with life insurance business in multi-line companies, sells comprehensive automobile insurance. Property and casualty insurance people have tried to do something about the carnage. But even though they have to pay death or injury claims on people killed or injured in auto accidents, the life insurance companies haven't made a big or particularly intelligent effort to do much about safety. The highway-safety measures of the property and casualty insurers have been minuscule compared with the achievements of the police, the highway engineers, and the professional safety experts. Even the automobile companies have done more than the insurance people. They have produced cars that hold the road better and stop more quickly—although there is much dispute about the sturdiness of the modern car, which is made light in weight to conserve fuel.

The motorist often finds the talk of insurance people about highway safety confusing. Many motorists get the idea that the companies are interested in proclaiming dubious safety standards for drivers only as a means of getting higher rates and earning bigger profits. Many insurance companies have also been accused of encouraging inflation of property-liability claims arising from auto accidents, as a means both of winning higher rates and of getting a reputation for being liberal on claims because such a reputation can make it easier to sell policies.

Crime is an area in which the insurance industry has shown itself to be far from public spirited. Of late, the tremendous increase in arson has compelled the fire insurance companies to take a more resolute stand and give the police and fire marshals more support and cooperation. But far too many cases of fairly obvious arson are settled at high payouts without a struggle, and there is too much ugly gossip about complicity of insurance people in some of these smelly arrangements. Arsonists comprise a recognized criminal profession. A veteran fire department officer can usually tell if a building has been torched, no matter how well arsonists conceal their tracks.

The losses from arson are enormous. The insurance companies and the insurance trade press talk a lot about arson, but spreading information about firebugs seems to be as far as they are willing to go. You don't read about many arsonists actually going to trial, and you don't hear of many property owners being prosecuted by insurance companies because of suspicious fires.

Probably the most glaring and cruel example of the life companies' lack of public spirit was the way they took part in or countenanced the wholesale "redlining" of large areas of our biggest cities when urban decay became acute in the 1960's. Instead of trying to stem the blight that ravaged inner-city areas, the life companies accelerated the destruction by refusing to provide mortgage money to real estate people and builders who wanted to acquire the rundown properties and modernize or replace them. They just drew lines in red ink around huge areas on the city maps and decreed that within these bloody boundaries they would not lend a penny.

The life companies weren't the only redliners, but

they were in the forefront of this movement that created deserts of demolished or abandoned blocks of flats, small stores, and small factories such as the South Bronx in New York City and many other redlined urban areas. The few remaining buildings in these areas were gutted by fires set by vandals or became warrens inhabited by bands of dope pushers, other criminals, and social dropouts.

No one has been able to figure out a way to rebuild into viable neighborhoods these urban deserts created by redlining, that smug and selfish exhibition of contempt for humanity.

The impact on society of redlining extends far beyond the immediate depopulation of big neighborhoods. Thousands of small businesses that provided jobs for unskilled workers were wiped out. Industries in the more prosperous areas of the cities found it increasingly difficult to get workers because affordable rental housing was no longer available for the workers anywhere in the city. People were compelled either to leave the cities in search of work or to congregate in a few crowded ghettos. Many just went permanently on the welfare rolls.

So businesses in the more prosperous parts of the cities began to move out of town and even to go bankrupt in substantial numbers for lack of workers and customers.

City tax revenues shrank because so many buildings were abandoned or at least torn down to reduce taxes.

The social and economic changes of the late 1950's and the 1960's started the blight, but redlining turned it into a veritable cancer, and the life companies cooperated wholeheartedly in the redlining.

It can be argued that the assets of life companies are the assets of the policyholders. If this is so, then helping to build up those urban areas would have increased the assets of the tens of millions of policyholders and improved living conditions for the general population. Unfortunately, with ostrich-like lack of courage, most insurance company executives found it easier to get out the red pencil.

The insurance industry has long been criticized for dealing with burglars who rob jewelers and private individuals of fancy baubles with the sole idea of selling the loot back to the insurance company. No one knows just how widespread this practice is, but an insurance company can avoid paying off a two-hundred-thousand-dollar loss claim by buying the jewelry back from the burglar for perhaps sixty thousand dollars. The thief thus gets fifty percent more than the going rate of twenty cents on the dollar of appraised value that the ordinary "fence" will pay.

The insurance company thereby becomes an accessory to the burglary. The police know very well what is happening, but they can't do anything about it because everyone involved will lie under oath on the witness stand.

If maneuvered into admitting that such transactions take place, the insurance people will say that they are only acting to reduce the loss and are no more culpable than someone who offers a reward for the return of lost property with no questions asked. But the reward to the thief is enormous in these cases, and he or she is assured of escaping prosecution.

Some life insurance companies also become involved with criminals from time to time—for example, by entering into bribery deals to land big packages of business and by making large personal loans to shady characters, loans that often are illegal and utterly uncollectible. What kind of favors the life insurance companies can get in return for these loans varies a great deal, and the information rarely leaks out.

Never in the country's history have the life companies and their owners or top management cliques been in the vanguard of movements for social improvement. Far from taking any role in civil rights, they cooperated until after World War II with those reactionary elements who wanted to keep black people in subjugation. They were also by and large anti-Jewish in their personnel policies and dragged their feet as long as they could on social justice for females.

They did support the Prohibition movement early in this century. They are against alcoholism because an alcoholic is usually a poor insurance risk and an uncertain payer of premiums. But the companies have given not much more than lip service to the effort to solve the great narcotics evil of today. They have not faced up to this matter in an effective way.

The life companies and the other insurance companies contend that they are leaders in social progress because they provide so much mortgage money and contribute so much capital flow for industry. But they are paid very well for this, and they avoid the riskier loans that the commercial banks make.

Leaders of the industry have been less willing on the whole than other business and professional people to stand up and be counted publicly on important controversial issues. Consequently, much of their political activity has been clandestine; and clandestine political activity has traditionally been disreputable and corrupt in all societies.

This is not a pretty picture. It is high time that all the insurance companies began to realize that their huge financial power imposes on them the obligation of genuine social, economic, and political responsibility toward all

Americans—not just their own managements.

If the insurance companies would take a reasonable part of their self-serving efforts at maintaining their privileges and high rates and divert the energy to tackling the appalling problems of crime and narcotics addiction, they would perhaps justify their appeal for public support.

Take the matter of crime. The companies could very well send people into the schools to impress on children the terrible consequence of a tolerance of crime and the so-called street-wise society. More than that, they could take the lead in demanding a much-needed reform in our creaky and dilatory court procedures, which are presently heavily overbalanced in favor of the criminal and against the law-abiding citizens who are the victims of crime. They could stand up and demand more adequate police protection and better-trained police forces. They could demand that the victims of crime be assured the services of an attorney, the same way criminals are.

Because they already have good medical research departments, the life companies are in a particularly strong position to play a leading role in the struggle to free much of America's population from the pernicious grip of the avaricious narcotics peddlers. The drug epidemic in this country and its effect on families and children is the greatest plague that we have ever had. One would think that all the resources of the life insurance industry would come into to play to alleviate this scourge on future generations. Here again, the insurance people should go into our schools and talk to kids and give them straight and convincing information about the horrible perils of drugs.

What I have tried to say is that, for an industry that

is so dependent on the good will of the multitudes, a more energetic approach to helping our entire population would be well advised. Such action can only endear the industry rather than have it totally castigated, as surely it will be if the do-nothing policy continues.

Much criticism of the entire insurance industry has taken place in recent years. People power has shown itself in the state of California. The enactment of Proposition 103 is proof positive that the industry of insurance must do a better job for all Americans.

It can no longer afford to be "smug."

8. The Heavy Grip of Inflation

Inflation has warped and eroded the traditional concept of life insurance for many consumers . . . It has forced changes in the traditional product line and company structure that could wipe out the present agency system, force some life companies out of business, and compel the survivors to trim their sails and drastically change their way of doing business.

THE 1974 *TREND REPORT* of the Institute of Life Insurance was more than a confession of past and current sins. Although it was drafted before price rises reached annual levels of twelve and thirteen percent under President Carter, it sounded the alarm that the industry was in grave danger from inflation.

The report said that solvency of the establishment companies was definitely threatened and that future operating costs would be unpredictable and unmanageable.

Over the long haul, the energy crisis was solved. Coal gasification, both underground and after the coal is brought to the surface, coal liquefaction, shale-oil extraction, massive production of renewable supplies of vegetable petroleum and ethanol alcohols, the fast-breeder nuclear reactor (which breeds more fuel than it consumes), and some applications of solar energy will do the job. There may be some help from light chemistry, too. But these are frightfully expensive, and we may not realize much from them for ten to twenty years.

Fortunately, Reaganomics and all of the economic philosophies of the Reagan administration did much to curb runaway inflation, reduce interest rates, and yet give our economy good grades during the past nine years.

The National Science Foundation issued a report on January 14, 1980, saying that although the global energy situation will cause difficulties for the United States, it need not slow the nation's long-term economic growth. But the foundation pointed out that we can hope for no miracles, that conservation must be our main defense, and that coal and nuclear fission must be relied on increasingly in the years ahead as natural petroleum becomes scarcer. Even though huge amounts of natural oil remain in the ground, much of it is inaccessible at any cost. The foundation study downgraded the outlook for solar energy substantially, saying that no ways to achieve economies of scale in producing it have been found or are likely to be soon, although the aggregate benefit of small solar-energy applications will be most useful.

Meanwhile, we are going to have to pay through the nose for gasoline, diesel fuel, and heating oil, and that will continue to run up the cost of housing, transportation, food, clothing—everything we require in our daily lives.

The Middle East situation is a drain on all the world except the communists, who profit by it. It's the prime cause of the high price and scarcity of oil. Of course, it can be said that the oil-exporting Arab countries are not being drained financially, but in reality they are. They maintain costly armaments, which they would not need if the Middle East crisis, now over thirty years old, could be solved. But countries not directly involved in the conflict between Israel and the Arabs, such as Turkey and Greece and even Pakistan, have had their economies disrupted by the long confrontation. Turkey is in the grip of severe inflation and an even worse energy shortage, which keeps her on the ragged edge of civil war.

Israel is undergoing fearful inflation. The mess in Iran, including the seizure of the hostages, was actually only a skirmish in the Middle Eastern conflict, humiliating as it was to Americans. In my opinion, the crux of the conflict is the demands of the Palestinians, which I do not think can be satisfied without destroying the state of Israel. Israel is not willing to commit suicide and the West is not willing to abandon Israel, but the communist countries and the more militant Muslim leaders seem determined to keep the conflict going until the end of this century.

The resumption of the cold war ran up American armament outlays and added to the difficulty of supporting the dollar and obtaining relief from inflation.

Despite its many gloomy prognostications for the future of life insurance, the *Trend Report* left out one of the most important reasons for pessimism. It failed to comment on the fact that the marvelous, almost miraculous scientific developments that helped the industry to prosper astoundingly in the years right after World War II are not likely to be duplicated in the remainder of the century.

The electronic-accounting revolution has not fully run its course, but the great cost and labor saving benefits to the life insurance companies already have been realized. And although medicine, surgery, and pharmaceutical chemistry will continue to advance, progress is sure to be much slower than during the war years and postwar years that gave humankind the antibiotic drugs and so many other blessings.

The consensus of opinion is that there is not going to be a breakthrough in treatment of cancer or cardiovascular diseases. There definitely is no single cause of cancer or heart diseases, and there will be no miraculous prevention or cure for either. So the life companies cannot expect another tremendous improvement in mortality experience and human lifespans, which would produce new profits and break the heavy grip of inflation for at least a decade or two.

Yet all across America I observe that people are living longer, into their late 70's and 80's and many into their 90's. but this has had little effect on life insurance profits, because people at that age generally no longer have their life insurance because they are unable to afford premium payments.

A leveling off in population expansion also will limit the growth of the business.

Inflation's heavy bite on industry and commerce in general may seriously erode the investment income in other businesses, which is almost as important as policy revenues to the life companies.

The most dangerous characteristic of inflation is its

persistence. During the second term of President Nixon, we hoped that the close of the Vietnam war would bring an end to inflation and possibly a beneficial deflation, but that did not happen. In a very real sense, today's inflation is worse than the galloping inflation that ravaged Germany, France, Italy, and Austria in the early 1920's. Fantastic as the fall of those countries' currencies then was, the critical period was brief, and it was followed by years of relative monetary stability. But there seems to be no hope of stability anywhere on the horizon today.

With a dry casualness, the *Trend Report* says, "The rate of inflation will abort thrift as an achievable goal in the minds of the public."

What do these stilted words really imply?

They imply the widespread death of the hope of laying up anything for the future and the total or nearly total destruction of the American way of working and saving. This is exactly what is happening today, as this revision goes to press. Our rate of saving continues to fall below that of the populaces of virtually all other industrialized countries. No matter how much a family makes, or how hard its members work, by the time they pay taxes, provide food, shelter, and clothing, and pay for braces for little Johnny's teeth, they have very little money left over to throw away on things that are not necessities of life. Now, more than ever, they cannot afford to waste precious dollars on cash value life insurance, or on any type of modified cash value policy that costs several times as much as low-cost term insurance, yet offers them a pitiful return on their so-called "investment."

The words of the *Trend Report* reflect a fear or at least a cynical belief that most Americans will turn to day-to-day opportunism or, like the people of so many underdeveloped countries, will come to believe that a government job is the only sure way of making a comfortable living. Now matter how you gloss it over, holding a government job means living off money sweated out of the taxpayers; it means the opposite of being productive. The *Trend Report* also hints at resulting problems within the life insurance industry that have an impact for future policyholders.

Professor Paul Pfeiffer of Kent State University in Ohio commented on one aspect of the problem in an address to the 1979 annual conference of the Life Management Society. He said that the 1980's would bring many employment problems for the life companies. He said that workers would want faster promotion and a bigger voice in management decisions but then added somewhat pessimistically, "yet their demands won't always coincide with commitment to greater quality work."

The *Trend Report* had plenty to say about employee relations. It said that inflation will force curbs on fringe benefits for workers and the pressure for shorter working hours will abate. It said that the companies will have to follow different philosophies in dealing with clerical and professional workers. The professional workers, being highly mobile and able to switch readily from company to company, will be interested in compensation solely on the basis of merit, the report said, but for clerical and other "inferior workers," it said, "the focus will be on cost-of-living incentives."

The report warned, though, that raising the compensation of "inferior" workers because of inflation's impact on the cost of living is sure to lead to discontent and a lack of motivation on the part of the "superior" workers.

That's a classic inflation dilemma that is being aggravated this time because the inflation is so persistent.

This is not hard to understand. We have drained all motivation out of tens of millions of our workers and have eliminated their self-respect over the last twenty-five years through giveaway programs that include unreasonable benefits in poverty checks, food stamps, and unemployment insurance on excessively easy terms.

We have seen in the previous chapters that many agents view with dismay the manner in which inflation is causing a shift from whole life to term insurance. They will have to sell a lot more death insurance to many more customers to make the same living, especially since inflation is also running up their living costs and their office and sales costs.

The *Trend Report* says that there will have to be some radical changes in the compensation of agents. It suggests, for example, that some of the indexed-commission-schedule methods used for property and casualty insurance could be adapted to life insurance and that perhaps salary should be a bigger portion of agents' compensation. On the indexing, the *Trend Report* suggests, "The type of indexing currently used for casualty coverage (such as regular or intermittent offers to increase homeowners' insurance as property values go up, the decrease in collision coverage as auto values to down) could be used for life insurance, possibly without the direct intervention of the agent, thus obviating the need for a full front-end (commission) load."

Another suggestion, put rather vaguely in the report, is for salaried agents.

However, it seems plain that an energetic, well-informed agent can do a lot to cope with the changing picture just by trying to make sure that his or her customers have as much death protection as they need and can afford. The need for death protection increases at least as fast as the inflation of money.

We have already pointed out that most couples in their prime years need at least $100,000 to $1 million worth of term death coverage. A family that needed and could afford $100,000 worth of insurance in 1967 may very well now need—and be able to afford—$300,000 worth of proper term death insurance.

Life insurance people also worry, with good cause, lest some consumers decide in these inflationary days to be "self insured," that is, to depend on their ability to save and invest their money for a maximum return instead of buying insurance. If you have been brainwashed into thinking of life insurance primarily as a way of saving, that would seem to make a lot of sense. But life insurance is not a way of saving. As I keep pointing out, it is death insurance. With proper term insurance, a couple with young children can accumulate an immediate $100,000 to $1 million estate for the family, if the breadwinner dies. There is simply no way this family could create such an estate by putting money in the bank and making a few modest investments.

This is where an honest advisor is worth his or her weight in gold. Honest advice on financial planning for the future of your family and yourself is covered in detail in a later chapter.

Unless the life companies adapt more rapidly than they have so far to the troubles caused by inflation, some of them are going to go under. As a matter of fact, I won't be surprised to see at least half of the 2,000 life insurance companies in existence today go out of business by the year 2000. The state insurance commissioners will probably compel the stronger companies to take over policies of companies facing collapse. That has been done for many years. Fortunately, as I pointed out earlier, most states now protect policyholders. But the stockholders and employees and many agents of the failing companies could be wiped out.

As this book revision occurs, I am happy to report that during the eight years of the Reagan presidency, the inflation rate in the United States went down to a respectable three to four percent per annum. This spectacular turnaround from the high rate of inflation during the Carter Administration of twelve to thirteen percent came in spite of President Reagan's insistence on a strong defense posture.

Yet this reduction in inflation should in no way encourage holders of obsolete policies to retain them.

9. The Bear Market Is Here

*The present is no time to buy life insurance stocks . . .
The thin market . . . The gloomy Chase Econometrics
Forecast . . . The plums have been picked . . . The loom-
ing personnel problems. Mutual funds for the average
investor.*

IN THE 1940's AND 1950's, some people made large profits by investing in the stocks of life insurance companies, because the business expanded so much in those years and the profitability was enhanced by a large increase in the average lifespan in America.

But even in the years when the business was having its greatest growth, the stocks of life companies required great patience on the part of investors if substantial rewards were to be reaped.

Although the shares of some of the big multi-line insurance companies are listed and traded on the New York Stock Exchange and a few life companies are listed

on the American Stock Exchange, the typical life
insurance company is closely held, and the minority
shares in the hands of the public are traded over the
counter. The market for these shares is usually somewhat
thinner than the market for shares of industrial companies
traded over the counter. That makes the life stocks rather
volatile and unsuited for the investor who wants to specu-
late on short term profits—the person who maintains
what is called in Wall Street a trading account with his or
her brokerage house, as distinguished from an investment
account.

The unsuitability of life insurance company stocks for
quick sale without the risk of a substantial markdown also
makes them somewhat difficult to borrow money on at the
bank. If you put up a hundred shares of General Motors
or some other respectable industrial stock as collateral for
a loan, the bank knows it can get its money in a matter of
hours or even minutes should you default. But it might
have to wait days to sell and collect on life stocks, and the
borrower would probably take a loss, and the bank might
lose some of its money.

Also, life insurance company shares have never been
considered income stocks. As a rule, they pay very modest
cash dividends or no dividends.

So stock life insurance companies have traditionally
paid dividends in stock, rather than cash. Thus, the only
way the buyer of the shares can reap cash from them is to
sell off his dividend shares from time to time or to sell his
holdings as their book value appreciates or to get paid for
them as the result of a merger or acquisition of the company. So the life stocks have been called growth stocks,
and their market value has depended on book value,
which is arrived at by dividing the number of shares

outstanding into the sum that the balance sheet indicates could be reasonably raised if the company's assets and business were sold.

A big attraction of all growth stocks is that if you make any profit by selling them, the profit is taxed as capital gains, rather than straight income, and taxes on capital gains are usually much lower than income taxes. In recent years, however, Congress has shown an inclination to raise the capital-gains tax rates, and that could make life insurance stocks and other growth stocks less attractive.

In the twenty-five years since the prices of life stocks peaked out and began to decline in 1964, their performance as growth stocks has left much to be desired.

But there now appear to be some comparatively new reasons for concluding that a bear market in life insurance stocks will remain with us for some time.

In the first place, we can see the working out of many of the difficulties forecast under Scenario 1 of the 1974 *Trend Report* of the Institute of Life Insurance.

Next, inflation obviously hurts the life insurance business more than it hurts other businesses. The life companies cannot raise prices to match inflation as manufacturers and producers of raw materials and commodities can, for the simple reason that they have been overcharging their customers for years and the inflation catches them at a time when the consumerist movement and competition are forcing them to cut prices. Their only resort is to sell more, and that can be a big order. The easiest way to sell more is to diversify into property and casualty insurance and investment instruments, but that entails much effort and acquiring much new knowledge and experience on the part of sales organizations.

Happily, many insurance agents have already acquired the necessary knowledge and experience. The "money doctor," more fully described in chapter 13, will become more and more a valuable asset to many insurance companies.

Another good reason this is not a good moment to invest in life stocks is that so many of the best companies, the real plums, have been swallowed up in mergers and acquisitions in the past few years. They have mostly been bought for stock, and the acquisition cost has diluted the shares of the purchasing companies and weakened their potential as growth stocks.

The life companies have successfully blocked the Federal Trade Commission for the moment from further investigation of their business, but the demands from consumerists for tighter regulation are rising. That is a threat to the value of life stocks that could choke off new investor interest.

Perhaps the most serious single problem for the companies was stated succinctly. even though he did not elaborate much on it, by Professor Paul Pfeiffer, of Kent State University, when he said that it is likely to be very difficult to motivate life insurance agents and employees in the 1980's. Michael Lynch, chief of the group of economists who worked on the controversial FTC staff report, took a similar view. He said that the people who may be the most shocked by an effective disclosure system could be the army of agents working for the establishment companies. He said that many of these agents may revolt when they learn that the companies have been requiring or inducing them to sell outmoded products for so many years.

The fact that the big mutual companies still have

such a large share of the market and are stronger financially in general than the stock life companies could also seriously hurt the prospects for the life stocks. In the booming forties and fifties, the stock companies greatly improved their share of the market, but that was mainly because they were able, through high-pressure selling and innovative policy designing, to expand the overall market rapidly. In a market that is not expanding rapidly, competing with the mutuals could be much harder, especially since the mutuals have been encroaching on the stock companies' own turf.

Many of the smaller companies are very marginal, but those which have carved specialties for themselves may survive; the others will be taken over by bigger companies. Lynch also said that the pressure for more regulation of the business will speed the shakeout. The companies' whole life insurance business will inevitably decline, and there will be ever-sharper attacks by consumerists on such profitable fields as credit life insurance and industrial life insurance—that is, small policies sold at high rates on monthly payments.

Also, there seems to be an exceptional interest in a few companies that are unusually successful in marketing term life insurance with mutual funds. These few companies should be watched carefully by potential investors for major growth potential.

While some have profited from life insurance stocks, investment in this area is best left to professional portfolio managers and investment gurus. For the average investor, however, mutual funds, well managed, are generally the best way to invest in a growing America while taking advantage of the "pooled" investment money of mutual funds to reduce the risk factor.

10. The $50 Billion Crock of Poppycock

The AIDS panic in America . . . Capitalizing on hysteria for profit . . . Another classic case of the insurance industry "sticking it" to the American consumer.

IT IS TIME for the life insurance industry to bring to an end the senseless era of panic that exists in America today.

The perpetrators of this Great American Propaganda Machine have brought millions of people to their knees in fear of an alleged AIDS epidemic which, as the life insurance industry would have you believe, could wipe out the entire U.S. population by the year 2000.

Poppycock.

What we have here is another classic case of the life insurance industry sticking it to the consumer one more time. The largest industry in the world—which will stop at nothing to become an even larger dinosaur—is using the overpublicized AIDS crisis to its own advantage.

That's right, you won't see any companies going out of business due to an overwhelming number of AIDS death claims. Instead, you will more likely see an across-the-board rate hike, blamed on (you guessed it) AIDS.

The industry's latest cry is that it will lose $50 billion in AIDS-related death claims on life insurance already in force.

So what if the industry does lose $50 billion to AIDS? Why not tighten controls on underwriting, take a look at increasing productivity or cut overhead to absorb the loss?

No. The insurance industry would prefer, instead, to make the consumer pay—and pay—and pay—all under the guise of a "national panic" created by none other than the life insurance industry itself.

Let's take it one step further by looking at just exactly who will be doing the paying: Mr. Middle America, that's who. He has little in common with the average AIDS victim, 73% of whom are male homosexuals, another 17% former intravenous drug users.

Back in 1945 when I entered the insurance business, a very common joke was that if you became disabled or died because you were gouged by a bull, you would have no trouble collecting on your insurance policy. But the insurance industry was so concerned about itself, even then, that there was a war clause in each policy that would disallow payment if death occurred due to an act of war.

As it turned out, so few deaths occurred that were war-related compared to the total mortality during the war period that insurance companies decided to pay those claims anyway. But why not learn something from the past? Why not put an AIDS clause in every policy that is issued in America today? Wouldn't that make more sense than raising the rates of millions of Americans?

The real kicker, however, is that while the industry will be jacking up its already inflated prices to make up for the alleged $50 billion loss, insurance companies will be reaping a mortality bonanza on the side. That's right, the now infamous $50 billion loss will be more than offset by decreased mortality. Coronary deaths are down 30% over the last decade, a statistic which rings big dollars in the insurance industry's oversized cash register.

The dollar signs may loom even bigger with recent FDA approval for a new drug to revolutionize the treatment of high cholesterol, thus cutting the risk of heart disease. It's unlikely, however, that you'll see insurance companies decrease their rates due to the decreased mortality.

But let's forget about idle speculation on what might happen in the future. Instead, I'd prefer to examine the facts as they are.

As of July 27, 1987, AIDS had claimed 22,548 lives since its discovery in 1980—a minuscule fraction of the U.S. population, to be sure. Despite what you might have heard on TV or read in your local newspaper, AIDS has not been the rampant killer some people (the life insurance industry heading that list) would have you believe.

For example, 24,000 died in alcohol-related auto accidents last year alone.

Now, don't get me wrong. I'm not saying that AIDS is not a serious issue—it is and it should be closely monitored. But life insurers are playing on the fear of the

American public and supporting the AIDS panic for one reason, and one reason alone: they want to justify yet another major hike to their already exorbitant rates. Yet AIDS death claims have hardly made a dent in the traditional life insurance industry's gold mine.

Take, for example, Prudential, the "rock" of the industry, a company that openly flaunts its assets, which surpass $130 billion. In 1986, Prudential had 135,000 death claims totalling $807 million. Only 225 of those claims were AIDS-related, costing Pru only $3.4 million.

New York Life, another self-hyped industry giant, paid only 0.8% of its claims for AIDS-related deaths. The industry, as a whole, reported about 1% of its $19.6 billion in death claims were caused by AIDS—the alleged life insurance company "Public Enemy Number 1."

Ridiculous.

It's easy to see why not everyone agrees with the industry when it promotes the AIDS hysteria. Chairman and Chief Executive Officer of Capital Holding, Thomas C. Simons, says the near-term public health threat posed by the disease has been "significantly" exaggerated. "Certainly, if it became a much more widespread threat, it could become a big problem for the insurance industry in 1995 or 2000," he said. "But at the moment, it's a yell in a windstorm."

Dan Rather recently interviewed Dr. Don Desjarlais on the CBS evening news. "We risk a real backlash if we try to scare everybody and then it turns out that that scare was not based on the real likelihood of transmission (of AIDS)," Desjarlais told the national television audience.

Of more than 38,000 Americans currently suffering from AIDS, only two percent are heterosexuals. Almost all these victims are women who got AIDS from men who used drugs or were bisexual.

Officials at the Center for Disease Control in Atlanta and elsewhere find no evidence that AIDS will reach epidemic proportions, except among homosexuals and intravenous drug users. As a consequence, there is growing consensus among leading medical scientists that the threat of AIDS to the wider population, while serious, has been exaggerated.

The bottom line is this: AIDS has yet to prove itself as the number one menace to society. A State Farm public relations specialist was recently quoted as saying, "We really don't know what to expect." If that's the case, and the industry admits it is, why make the consumer pay, not to mention panic?

Now the industry is crying that hundreds of insurance companies will go out of business due to AIDS-related death claims. The truth is, 500 to 700 companies will become insolvent between now and the year 2000—not from AIDS, but from mismanagement, selling the wrong products and deceiving the American public.

11. *The Industry's Mistakes*

The unjustified mystique . . . Wasteful children's insurance . . . Too many rogues . . . The policy-loan-interest racket . . . Poor agent selection and training . . . Unjust restrictions on policy replacement

FROM ITS EARLIEST DAYS, the life-insurance industry has been less willing than other businesses to admit its mistakes. Having adopted a posture of being marvelous new benefactors of humankind, its leaders felt bound to assume a mystique of infallibility such as the leaders of religions often feel compelled to profess.

Of course, the truth is quite different. The business was founded in an era of brutal *caveat-emptor* economics, and the Brahmans who run the establishment life companies in the United States have attempted to maintain this "let the buyer beware" philosophy well into the last quarter of the twentieth century. They are being fooled, however. The educated consumer of the 1980's and 1990's has changed that old caveat, "Let the buyer beware," to a new one, "Let the competition beware."

Most of the industry's errors have been at the expense of the insurance-buying public, but not altogether so. Wasteful management and extravagance and bad judgment in investments can be as harmful to life-company stockholders as to policyholders. It is the duty of state regulatory officials to look for such abuses and expose them. They do this a little more frequently than is generally realized, but actual prosecution occurs only in the more flagrant cases, and many insurance people believe that the establishment companies are dealt with leniently. On the other hand, agents can be subjected to considerable regulatory harassment if they behave in a way that is offensive to the establishment.

One of the earliest mistakes of the industry was to encourage the sale of life insurance on children. In an age when childhood diseases caused high mortality rates, it was easy to sell parents on the idea of insurance that would at least pay the funeral expenses when a child died. And there was the added sales argument that an early policy would give the child lifelong insurability protection.

This backfired. Childhood mortality rates and suspicious deaths of children went up surprisingly on both sides of the Atlantic. The losses to the companies were heavy. That did not stop the companies from pushing the sale of insurance for children; it only made them sell more selectively. As late as the early 1930s, millions of families burdened themselves to buy whole life insurance on their children instead of purchasing death insurance for the father, the family breadwinner. Even endowment policies for children were sold on the idea that they would come due and be paid off in time to provide useful funds in the critical young-adult years. The truth, of course, is that even then there were vastly better ways to save money for children than buying such expensive life-insurance policies on them.

Greed and duplicity have been the life-insurance industry's greatest sins. Sins are mistakes; in church and synagogue, congregations confess in their prayers, "We have erred grievously in thy sight, O Lord." As early as 1877, Elizur Wright, a Massachusetts mathematician who later became the state's first insurance commissioner, wrote a little book entitled *Traps Baited with Orphans.* Wright exposed the shortcomings of whole-life cash-value insurance roundly and concluded, "I became convinced that life insurance was the most available, convenient and permanent breeding place for rogues that civilization ever had presented."

That things haven't changed altogether since Wright's day could be inferred from a recent popular detective novel. The villain in the story is a vice-president of a life-insurance company. Early on, he remarks rather cheerfully to a claims investigator, "[Owning] a life insurance company is a license to steal."

One of the worst examples of company greed that betrays the uninformed policyholder into making serious mistakes is the policy loan. Instead of conceding you the right to withdraw some of the surplus premiums you have paid on a whole-life cash-value policy, the companies pretend that they are lending you money and charge you interest on it. They get away with this, and state insurance codes actually define this withdrawal of your own money as a loan. At present the companies are moaning that the interest rates on these loans aren't high enough, and we saw in the chapter on the 1974 *Trend*

Report that they were even talking of welshing on guarantees of loan-interest rates written into the new policies.

A couple of years ago, the establishment companies prevailed on state insurance commissioners to increase interest on loans made to policyholders (of their own money) from an average of five percent to eight percent. With few exceptions, industry executives flocked together and, regardless of the impact on the public, followed the lead in carrying out this outrageous imposition.

It used to be much more sensible most of the time for the policyholder to borrow money elsewhere rather than from the insurance company. At least he or she would be getting the use of extra funds instead of paying for the privilege of using his or her own money. But probably, policy loans are usually taken out because the insured is in no position to borrow from a bank or finance company at the moment.

On the whole, policy loans have been fabulously profitable to life companies. In times when bank and finance-company rates were low, interest rates on life-insurance-policy loans were comparatively low.

Careless selection and poor training of salespeople is a mistake the life-insurance business has made in common with many other businesses. For years most or many salespeople rose from the ranks of the debit or industrial-life forces. This is the business of ringing doorbells, or visiting factories during lunch hours, to sell small policies of a few hundred dollars to the lowest-income workers, to be paid for by the month. The salespeople build up collectible accounts called debits and have to call every month and collect the small premiums themselves.

Their customers are not sophisticated, and it is not at all hard to sell them small amounts of insurance at rates three and a half to five times as high as the rates that would be quoted middle-class life-insurance prospects. Over the years there have been many exposés of industrial life insurance but it still goes on. For many years this was almost the only life insurance available to blacks, and I am told that in the Deep South it was called bluntly "nigger insurance." As was the case (and still is sometimes) with other commodities and services, the poor blacks were charged several times as much for paltry insurance protection as upper-working-class and middle-class whites would pay for much better protection.

This debit insurance is not sold by small, disreputable companies as a rule. The greater part of the business is written by the big establishment companies.

Salespeople trained in that rapacious and cynical field were not likely to become oversolicitous about policyholders or too squeamish about gouging them for every penny of commissions they could squeeze from them.

Things have improved in recent years. Agents are somewhat better trained, but the training is still aimed at maximizing commission earnings and company profits, not at giving policyholders maximum death protection for their survivors for the least money.*

Stringent underwriting has caused many persons to buy "rated" policies because of supposed health or occupational perils, forcing them to pay extra dollars in premiums over the years. These rated health and occupational hazards have been shown to be highly overrated and not to justify so much in premiums. But the companies have not made any effort to rectify these ratings and reduce the premiums—another industry mistake that will arouse

*See Arthur Milton, *How to Get a Dollar's Value for a Dollar Spent* (Secaucus, N.J.: Citadel Press, 1964).

public resentment.

The duplicity of the life companies was most glaring in the arcane language in which they wrote their policies, language so obfuscating that even an attorney could not comprehend it unless he or she had specialized in insurance law. The insured had to take their agents' word for what the policy said, and there were plenty of occasions when a beneficiary learned that the policy did not say what the agent had pretended it did when he or she sold it. Not until the early 1970s did harsh criticism from many quarters force a few of the companies to start writing their life policies in plain English. Before this, even the sales organizations had often not known how to read the policies.

Life-insurance companies can be extremely alert and forward looking when new opportunities develop for profit, either in selling policies with new wrinkles to the public or in making investments with handsome yield potential. But they show a curiously ostrich-like attitude toward really important and widespread social changes. It seems to me that the establishment companies have kept their heads buried in the sand for the past fifteen years while the tides of consumerism rose all around them and threatened ultimately to engulf them completely.

They keep on stubbornly increasing their efforts to maintain expensive sales forces devoted to selling products that not only are outdated but, in many cases, should never have been offered for sale in the first place.

But from the standpoint of both the public and the insurance agents, the worst mistakes of the companies have been to frustrate legitimate regulation of the industry by the states. They have effectively pigeonholed the state insurance laws and turned them and the state insurance officials largely into instruments to protect the companies instead of the public.

The most glaring example of this is the way the anti-twisting rules have been turned into means of locking policyholders into high-cost cash-value insurance policies that no longer serve the needs of the insured but still earn fat profits for the companies. The states originally adopted the anti-twisting rules to stop agents from shifting policies from company to company or even shifting customers to other policies in the same company just to generate fat commissions. This practice was analogous to unscrupulous stockbrokers' "churning" customers' stocks portfolios in order to generate commissions.

But as the public became better informed and the number of sophisticated insurance agents increased, the companies persuaded the state insurance departments to turn the anti-twisting rules into newer, tougher "replacement regulations" designed to make it more difficult for a private individual to change her or his insurance and to make it unprofitable and even illegal and dangerous for an agent to help a customer get out of a bad life-insurance situation and into a good one.

Suppose John Appleseed, who lives in New York State, has a hundred thousand dollars' worth of very old cash value insurance written at a time when mortality experience was a lot poorer than it is now, investment-income prospects were not as good, and premiums were much higher. He asks his agent what to do.

The agent knows full well that he can get Appleseed a hundred thousand dollars' worth of term insurance for not more than one-sixth of what he is paying now, all things considered. The cash-value policy or policies can be cashed in for, say, fifteen thousand dollars, and this sum

can be put in a savings bank or otherwise invested to earn
10 percent, as against the yield from the cash-value policy
on premiums paid in of from 1½ to 4 percent.

But because of Regulation 60 of the New York State
Department of Insurance, put into effect in October 1971,
the agent is going to be awfully wary about advising
Appleseed to take this sensible step. The commission on
the new arrangement for Appleseed might be less than
$150, and Regulation 60 forces the agent to go through
complicated steps that eat up much of the commission in
clerical costs. Also, if he makes a small mistake, or even if
he merely incurs the displeasure of the company that now
insures Appleseed or its agent, he can be harassed and
fined by the state insurance department and even have his
license revoked.

As a former insurance commissioner once told me,
this regulation is the biggest vote for high-cost insurance
ever perpetrated on the public by the establishment.

Ever since the replacement problem began nibbling
at the entrenched privileges of the establishment companies, they have been putting pressure on all state
insurance departments to adopt similar rules. They have
succeeded in virtually all the states. This has been done
very quietly. These tough new rules haven't had to be
voted on by the state legislatures, and hardly anyone outside the industry knows about them. Only a handful of
agents so far have been willing to stick their necks out and
protest.

The antireplacement rules are all proceeded by pious
declarations that they are designed to protect the public,
but if you ask a *former* state insurance official about it,
the chances are he or she will tell you bluntly that the
rules are designed to protect the companies, not the

public. Of course, these regulations also say that a private individual can change his or her insurance if he or she wants to, but there are some big catches to it. It is difficult, almost impossible, to buy standard term life insurance at reasonable prices without going through an agent, and you usually have to prove that you are still medically insurable. If you cash in your existing insurance first so you can buy new insurance without going through complicated "replacement" procedures, you are left in the meanwhile without death protection, and there is the risk that you might be turned down medically for the replacement insurance.

To give you an idea of how ridiculous the regulation is, it talks about the suicide clause and the contestable period you would have in a new policy that you don't have in the old policy. Generally, the suicide and contestable clauses run for two years and then expire. Can you imagine that the combined genius of the life-insurance executives and state insurance officials has caused them to conclude that you might commit suicide in the next two years or you will commit fraud in your application for the new policy? How sad it is that these attitudes have served to make the public even more wary of the life companies.

As a rule, the tough replacement regulations don't apply to group insurance, insurance issued as part of a pension plan, or nonrenewable term insurance. But the New York rule applies to "any replacement transaction which involves annuity contracts except those provisions which require the completion and furnishing of a disclosure statement."

New York Regulation 60 is a fourteen-page document that ends with a dozen detailed admonitions that must be given to applicants who want to change their insurance, warning them that doing so is nearly always a bad thing. It is a defense of whole-life cash-value insurance all the way and doesn't contain a single phrase about the advantages of term insurance or the need for a maximum death benefit. The agent is required to furnish this document to people like John Appleseed.

The agent is also required by Regulation 60 to fill out a whole series of disclosure forms listing all Appleseed's life-insurance policies, the policy numbers, the companies' names and addresses, the face amounts, the various benefits and options, and the premium rates, with tables of dividend and cash-value prospects for each policy for many years hence. The agent also must give specific reasons for dropping each old policy and specifying the advantages to be obtained by purchasing the new policy. These forms must be signed by both the agent and Appleseed. Copies of them must be sent to all the insurance companies involved, as well as to all the other life-insurance agents Appleseed has dealt with. All this runs into time and money.

Regulation 60 also provides severe penalties for any agent for "counselling of the insured to write directly to the company in such a way as to bypass such company's agency representation or obscure the identity of the replacing agents and company."

In the closing statement's admonitions that have to be given to Appleseed, Regulation 60 contains this advice: "For your protection, you should receive the comments of the present insurance company before arriving at a decision on this important financial matter."

Possibly, but if Appleseed drives a Ford and decides to trade it in on a Chevrolet, would state officials presume to tell him he should ask the advice of the Ford Motor

Company and the state motor-vehicle department before closing the deal?

The establishment life companies would doubtless answer that you don't buy an automobile to keep for life and expect it to increase in value. But in this inflationary era we have seen that old life-insurance policies lose their value, and the companies admit that. But more important, the average life of a life-insurance policy that stays in effect is now less than the average life of a good automobile. Recent industry figures tell us that when people are sold that newfangled universal life insurance policy, some 23% get rid of it in the first 24 months.

So Regulation 60 and rules like it in other states seem more and more like arbitrary abuses of regulatory power to aid and protect the life-insurance establishment.

12. The Disclosure Fiasco

The industry's poor public image . . . Deliberate deceptions . . . The widows study . . . The NAIC disclosure-plan hoax . . . Failure of the huge public relations effort to tell people what they need to know.

I AM PROBABLY MORE CONCERNED than anyone else I know about the life insurance industry's public image. After all, this is the industry in which I have spent forty-five years of my life, the industry that has been so kind to me, yet so thoughtless to consumers at large. Yet there's no doubt, as this book goes to press, that the life insurance industry has a serious image problem, and it is equally true that it is the industry itself that is responsible for that poor image.

In 1975, the news magazine *U.S. News and World Report* published a wide-ranging study of American opinion. One of the conclusions it published was that only about nineteen percent of those queried said they thought the life insurance companies deserved a good rating for providing the public with information. Things have not changed much in the intervening fifteen years.

Considering the large public relations and publicity efforts the industry has mounted all through this century, that was a rather devastating verdict. It implied that the life companies' boasted disclosures about their business look to the public like a fraud.

Is it because executives of life companies have acted holier-than-thou and have always felt that they were running charitable institutions, which, in fact, they have not been doing at all?

The companies practice bold deceptions. I spoke about the gall of the companies in making you pay interest on your own money when you take out a policy loan. But if you don't take out a loan and continue to pay level premiums on a cash value policy, you pay the same price year after year for less and less death insurance. Suppose you have a twenty-thousand-dollar policy that costs five hundred a year. The first year you paid five hundred for twenty thousand dollars' worth of death protection. But suppose that now your policy has accumulated eight thousand dollars in cash value. You are really paying five hundred per year now for only twelve thousand dollars' worth of death protection. This is rarely disclosed by the agent selling the policy. In fact, he or she may even mislead the applicant into thinking the survivor will get the twenty thousand dollars plus the accumulated cash values if the applicant dies, which isn't the case. She or he will get twenty thousand dollars, less any loan the insured may have taken out on the policy. Your so-called "investment portion" (cash values) is lost upon your death.

In 1970, the Life Underwriter Training Council and the Life Agency Management Association published a study based on interviews in 1968 and 1969 with about 1,750 recently widowed women. It was called *The Widows Study*.

The results of that study were shocking, and exposed the fiasco of protecting your loved ones that the life insurance companies had been selling for decades. Although ninety-two percent of the widows said that their husbands had some kind of life insurance, seventy percent got death benefits of less than ten thousand dollars and fifty-two percent less than five thousand dollars. Only seven percent received monthly payments under policy options. Yet forty-seven percent of these widows had dependent children. Half of them said their standards of living had dropped fairly sharply after their husbands died. This pathetic showing reveals something radically wrong with the business of life insurance.

Perhaps the most remarkable discovery in the study was that only twenty percent of these women had seriously discussed life insurance with their husbands or an insurance agent and many of them had no idea how much insurance there was in the family until the husband and father died.

Of course, in the nearly two decades since that study, things have changed. The working wife is the rule in America now, and the life insurance companies, who fifty years ago were extremely reluctant to insure females, are eagerly trying to sell them policies, because on the average, women live about seven years longer than men. So women know a lot more about life insurance, and husbands nowadays rarely make a life insurance decision without telling their wives all the details and asking their advice.

This improvement doesn't excuse the cruel hoax that the life insurance establishment perpetrated on people for a hundred and fifty years in pretending that whole life cash value insurance generally provided anything substantial for a man's wife and children if he died young. This was the first great disclosure fiasco of the industry.

What I am getting at is simply that the cost of ten thousand dollars' worth of whole life insurance is almost the same as the cost of a hundred thousand dollars' worth of term insurance, and probably the latter is what the industry always should have offered the public. This is even more true today, because, as I have already revealed, taxation and inflation have made it hard enough for most folks just to make ends meet. They just about have enough dollars left over for pure, unadulterated death insurance. Yet the traditional companies continue to sell whole life insurance, and the results of the 1970's widows study remain, tragically, too much of a reality as we enter the 1990's. (Remember that I said in chapter one that in 1987, the average size death claim of all life insurance companies in the U.S. was a paltry $7,050! How little progress the industry has made.)

In the last chapter I described another disclosure fiasco, the antireplacement regulations that employ complicated so-called disclosure procedures to lock policyholders into bad insurance situations and tie the hands of concerned agents who want to help the policyholders.

The conflict between the disclosure plan on true life insurance policy costs proposed in the 1979 FTC staff report and the disclosure plan drafted by the National Association of Insurance Commissioners was described in chapter 4. Peter Spielman and Aaron Zelman say in their book *The Life Insurance Conspiracy* that "the NAIC plan is so weak it is laughable."

After getting several states to adopt the NAIC disclosure plan, the life insurance lobby in Washington succeeded in 1978 in getting both House and Senate appropriations committees to put in the budget appropriation for the FTC these words: "The committee directs that in no event should the Commission or its staff attempt to impede or thwart the adoption by the states of the model life insurance cost solicitation regulation supported by the NAIC."

That tied the FTC staff's hands only through fiscal 1979. The controversial staff report was issued around the end of the fiscal year, and we have seen how the insurance industry then turned to tie the hands of the FTC staff again by getting the Senate Commerce Committee to adopt the Cannon insurance amendment to the McCarran-Ferguson Act.

Perhaps the worst disclosure fiasco is the idea harped on in much life insurance company propaganda that many persons lack the discipline to save their money themselves and the insurance companies are doing them a great favor by saving it for them—for a price. Even in days when people were not as well educated as now, there was very little truth in this propaganda. It is natural for people to save. The rustic who buried his money in the ground in a crock was acting out of ignorance and distrust of his fellows. The farmer's wife who kept her butter-and-egg money in a paper bag buried in the sugar jar was being foolish. But they both saved. And even in the nineteenth century there were savings banks, building-and-loan associations, and other thrift institutions where people could deposit their savings and have them grow and earn much more than a life insurance policy could accumulate.

Today the small-savings opportunities are numerous, and the poorest of them return a much better yield than a cash value life insurance policy.

The significant thing is that people have always demonstrated their eagerness to save. All they needed was opportunity and information. Even illiterate Americans would save to buy a little piece of land and put a house on it, or to get a horse or a cow or a piece of farm machinery. As people became more sophisticated, they learned how to borrow from banks for these things and how to plan to make them earn much more than enough to pay off the loan.

People also save through Christmas savings clubs and similar devices. Purchases of annuities, mutual funds, and investments (as distinguished from outright speculation) in stocks and bonds come largely out of savings.

The measure of Americans' ability to save on their own is the vast diversity and volume of savings. One need only review ordinary bank deposits, money market fund accounts, mutual fund purchases, the vast monies in bank CD's, to realize that the old staid life insurance company propaganda—that you need them to help you save your money—does not exist, if ever it did.

There's another side to the story: We now have in the United States, as a result of inflation, an "underground" economy that some good economists think is at least one-third as large as the recorded economy. The personal savings that grow out of this underground economy go highly unrecorded and are at a higher percentage of income than the recorded savings because they so frequently escape being taxed. If we could include the savings growing out of the underground economy in the national personal-savings statistics, it is fairly certain the figure would be much higher than the 4.8 percent figure recorded for 1986.

That 4.8 percent is a sorry figure, one of the lowest current rates of any developed country, and it says volumes about the careless economic policies we have been following as a nation in recent years. But even that figure is so big that it demonstrates the total falsehood of propaganda that people need a life insurance company to stand over them and make them save.

Another disclosure failure is the neglect of the life companies to tell their agents or even the agency supervisors the whole truth about the industry or even about the company they are working for.

Many universities now have professors who teach insurance as an important part of business economics, and considerable about it is taught in the better high schools. In spite of this, some surveys made by life insurance trade groups in recent years have shown that fully half of all agents and probably a much higher proportion of captive agents have totally erroneous ideas about the true nature of the business. One fairly extensive study made by the National Association of Life Underwriters and the Life Insurance Marketing and Research Association found that thirty-seven percent of all full-time agents believe there is little or no difference between companies in the prices of similar policies, and another eleven percent said they didn't know anything about that.

Worse, the study showed that the supervisors were worse informed than the agents. Forty-five percent of the supervisors opined that there was very little difference in similar-policy premium costs, and eleven percent said they didn't know.

This flies right in the face of the demonstrable fact that no industry in America has such a widely varied, chaotic, and inexplicable pricing structure as life insurance.

If the agents and supervisors don't know the truth, how can they possibly disclose it to the public?

The enormous public relations and publicity effort of the life insurance business is carried on by both the individual companies and trade associations. Many of these activities are on a high plane and well done. Statistical information is gathered regularly and made available to the government and to educational and scientific bodies.

This information is voluminous and reliable. The health research and vital statistics reports of the industry are particularly good. So are the statistics on the industry's growth and profitability, gross benefits payments, investment income, and contribution to national capital formation.

But this avalanche of information is only another disclosure fiasco when it comes to telling the average family what it really needs to know about life insurance, how to get the most and best death protection for the least money, and how to avoid being sold a policy that turns out to be an expensive lemon and getting locked into it.

13. *Life Insurance: Are You Robbing Yourself?*

Life insurance in a nutshell . . . Keep it simple . . .
Financial planning taboo . . . You need a Ph.D. to help
you buy term insurance and invest the difference . . . The
universal life policy sham . . . Wounding the octopus.

IT'S AXIOMATIC that predators and sharp operators
in business, con men and burglars, thrive largely by taking advantage of the ignorance and carelessness and sometimes the greed and vanity of their victims.

If all of us would take prudent precautions habitu-
ally, a lot fewer persons would be swindled, burglarized
or held up, and if enough persons would take the trouble

to learn the elemental facts about life insurance before they buy policies, the voracious octopus I described in the beginning of this book soon would sicken and die.

I admit that it isn't easy for ordinary folk to learn the basic truth about life insurance because the establishment companies have a huge vested interest in making it difficult, and they have succeeded in muddying the waters and hiding the truth for a century and a half. Their latest effort to delude and confuse the public about life insurance is a monstrosity called the universal life policy, about which I will have more to say later in this chapter. It is another attempt to force consumers to rob themselves.

In a nutshell, life insurance is protection against a great hazard. What is that hazard?

It is the peril of early death.

But for a hundred and fifty years the industry has sold its policies as protection against ultimate death, which is not a hazard but a certainty, for we must all die sometime. Prudent persons prepare for ultimate death by living sensible lives and training their children to become self-supporting at a reasonable age and by accumulating savings and other assets to take care of themselves in their later years.

We need life insurance protection against the peril of early death only in our prime years and during these years we need the largest amount of life insurance possible for the smallest possible premium payments. Yet the life insurance industry has devoted itself to selling us the least possible protection for the highest premiums the traffic will bear and the biggest possible profit to the life companies and their agents.

The industry's chief tool in accomplishing this aim is

the whole life cash value policy which pretends to protect against the false hazard of ultimate death.

The overwhelming majority of persons do not need any financial protection against ultimate death. By the time they die, their basic obligations to their children will have been discharged. There are exceptions, of course; some elderly persons have invalid dependents for whom they cannot provide except by means of an insurance policy, and others in reduced circumstances may need a small policy to assure themselves a decent burial. For a few there may be special business or tax reasons for having insurance.

But nearly all of us need protection in our prime years so that, even if we are only earning twenty thousand dollars a year, we can leave our wives and children from $250,000 to $1 million if we die suddenly while still young. For persons in their late sixties or seventies the cost of such substantial protection by means of term life insurance is extravagant or even prohibitive. The money to pay the very high premiums can be better invested in other ways.

A large proportion of the over-priced, inadequate whole life policies now in effect have been sold on the false theory that insurance is cheaper, a tremendous bargain, if you buy it while you are very young. Of course, the premium is lower, but you will be paying it for an awful lot of years. The fact is that, in spite of the confusing variety of whole life policies and the astonishing differences in premium rates quoted by various companies for practically identical policies, it is generally true that the overall cost averages out the same over a normal life span, no matter at what age the policy is purchased. The youngster who buys at a low premium when he or she is twenty-one will pay just about the same amount for $25,000 in insurance as the person who buys at a much higher premium in his or her forties if both have about the same life span. The establishment company agents will admit this if pressed, but they still prey on the public's misinformation and mental carelessness to get people to buy insurance "while you're young because it's cheaper."

The fact is that very young single persons do not need life insurance protection except in some special circumstances.

An even worse delusion is the idea that by purchasing life insurance you can eat your cake and have it, that the protection doesn't cost much because sooner or later you or your beneficiary will get back virtually every cent you have paid in. This can happen, but it's not the usual experience. You generally pay a lot more than you get back.

Two facts will demonstrate the falsity of the "eat your cake and have it" delusion. One is that the accumulated cash values of a life policy are not added to the death settlement and the other is that a very high percentage of all whole life policies lapse comparatively early and all that has been paid in on them is gone.

No, life insurance is not a way of getting something for nothing, as I have pointed out in this and other books.

The notion that life insurance is a good way to save money also is a delusion and it can be a very expensive one. Practically any other type of well-recommended sound investment will return a significantly better yield.

So, the lesson on this is "keep it simple." Stick to term insurance.

If you adhere to the "keep it simple" maxim, you

soon will discover that for most of us the currently popular cult of the professional financial planner should be taboo. Undoubtedly, some of the members of this new, slightly esoteric profession are good, but finding one with a really impressive track record is likely to be quite difficult. Like all new professions, financial planning has attracted many persons who simply haven't made good at anything else.

However, the main reason a professional financial planner should be taboo is just that not enough of us need one. Modern life has a way of relieving most of us of the burden of planning our finances. Uncle Sam, the state, and perhaps the city take big bites out of our paychecks for income taxes. Sales and excise taxes and social security taxes grab another big chunk. Rent or mortgage payments and real estate taxes and the grocery budget come next. Gasoline, the car payment, automobile and property insurance, life insurance, health insurance, school bills, clothing, and a little entertainment and recreation leave us with too little discretionary income to warrant the attention of a good financial planner. Even a family with an income of $100,000 a year may not have enough to put in savings and investments to warrant the professional planner's services.

If a financial planner really is good and has the track record to prove it, he will charge rather high fees and it won't be worthwhile for him to bother with very small accounts. On the other hand, the kind of planner who has to take on little clients may be tempted to advise unnecessary financial activity in order to build up fees and commissions for himself. And remember, the planner's service fees must come on top of fixed commissions you must pay brokers and agents when buying insurance and buying or selling securities. The planner may also turn out to be the kind who thinks he has to do something unusual to impress his clients with his expertise and sophistication. That can be risky and expensive for the clients.

So, by engaging a small-time financial planner you may be robbing yourself to pay him.

The proof of competence and reliability in a financial planner lies in performance. Academic credentials are no guarantee of performance. Some persons are good at passing examinations, but are not good at making further use of the knowledge acquired. But academic credentials do show that the person has taken courses in the field and passed the exams. Trade or professional association credentials, on the other hand, may mean only that the person calling himself or herself a financial planner has sent a check to the association and asked to be enrolled.

Let us remember that financial planning is not yet a regulated profession, and if you lose money by listening to bad advice from a financial planner you may find you have little or no recourse against him and hardly any chance of recovering your money.

However, a number of colleges now are giving courses in financial planning and at least two recognized schools with good reputations devote their curriculums primarily to insurance and financial planning. American College at Bryn Mawr, Pennsylvania, which has been awarding degrees in life insurance training for fifty years, has added a full course in financial planning leading to a degree. Virtually all its first class of candidates for this degree were also graduates of the life insurance course. The other recognized institution specializing in the field is the College of Financial Planning in Denver.

There is one infallible way to eliminate from

consideration any candidate to be one's financial planner or even one's insurance person. The chap who tries to get you to sign on the dotted line for a cash value life insurance policy or for one of the gimmicky new universal life policies should be avoided like the plague.

What the ordinary Joe or Jill with two or three thousand dollars a year to save and invest needs instead of a financial planner is a Ph.D., not the kind of chap who wears black robes and lectures in academic halls, but a "Proper Honest Director" who will provide reliable guidance in choosing such sound but mundane investments as savings deposits, mutual funds and stocks and bonds. Traditional as all these investment and savings vehicles are, none of them are really simple. They come in astonishing variety and it is easy for the novice to make mistakes in selecting those best suited to his or her needs. It is even easier to make mistakes in setting up a tax-deferred savings and investment program such as an Individual Retirement Account or a Keogh Plan if you own a business or professional practice. Present laws and social and economic conditions are making IRA's and Keogh Plans imperative for a growing segment of Americans as a supplement or alternative to Social Security.

How can one get this Proper Honest Direction?

Mostly by one's own efforts. There are plenty of persons in business with the necessary expertise and the right incentives to give you honest advice and help in the hope of getting your business, but you must learn how to find these people. You must learn how to read and analyze their advertising carefully and to distinguish between the sales pitches the ad men put in the copy and the genuine information. You may have to work to find the right person to help you.

You will also have to read and study the basic principles of saving and investing. The book stores and libraries are full of competent works on the subject. Some of the books are very general; others are very specialized although written in clear, understandable English. There are plenty of newspaper, magazine and radio commentators giving advice for free. In all probability you can even find an evening course in personal financial management and investing at a local college.

But vital as all this personal learning can be, it is only the start of a successful process. You still need some expert direction when you get down to the nitty gritty of buying securities, deciding when to sell them, deciding when to switch savings deposits, setting up your IRA or Keogh Plan and buying term life insurance, annuities and mutual funds.

The life insurance agent probably will prove to be the key to opening the doors to Proper Honest Direction. The dramatic changes in the life insurance industry in recent years have made it necessary for the agent to diversify his business tremendously. He is no longer able to make a good living just selling life insurance. There is one important exception to this development that we'll talk about a little later on. But the life agent must also sell annuities and property and automobile insurance, and he probably also is involved in IRA's and Keogh Plans and mutual funds. If he can't give you expert advice on a particular security or other investment, he knows where to find the right expertise very quickly.

Insurance agents have diversified so much that many of them can provide nearly all the advice and services one could expect from a professional financial planner, and often they will do this for commissions and possibly a very modest fee. It may be wise to take a peek at what has happened to the life insurance agents to make them branch out so.

Between 1969 and 1979 the population of the United States grew by twenty-three million, yet the number of insurance agents stood virtually still and their share of the total insurance market—life, health and property/casualty (including automobile)—dropped from 80 percent to 45 percent. Things have not been improving since 1979.

Clearly, something must have gone wrong. Either the insurance agents no longer were giving their customers good service or they were pricing themselves out of the market. I think both mistakes were being committed. As long as the agents let themselves be brainwashed by the establishment life companies into continuing to sell over-priced whole life cash value policies that did not provide adequate protection for the family against the consequences of early death, they were not really serving their customers. And the longer they confined their activity to selling insurance, the farther the agents advanced along the road to pricing themselves out of the market. The history of American business, particularly the recent history, shows that almost no marketing systems can be supported by only one product or line of products. That may be the overriding reason why there has been so much diversification in every area of American business since World War II, and nowhere has the trend to diversification been more marked than in the financial service industries. We have seen big banks create one-bank holding companies that gave them the legal right to get into many new fields. We have seen Merrill Lynch, the biggest Wall Street house, open hundreds of offices selling a variety of services, including real estate management and executive relocation. We have seen Sears Roebuck sell every kind of insurance, stocks and mutual funds over the counter like paints and clothing. We have seen the largest of all sales organizations, A.L. Williams, in just twelve years, capture the imagination of millions of purchasers of term life insurance and mutual funds. Their basic philosophy of buying term and investing the difference has paid off handsomely for their clients and representatives alike.

And now we have to face up to the possibility that in the not too distant future people will buy insurance or stocks and bonds or IRA retirement plans through department stores or banks via two-way cable television and their home computer terminals.

This prospect raises a lot of questions for the insurance agents and for the public. For example, a lot of business has been lost by insurance people because of the dramatic rise of the so-called direct writing of property/casualty policies sold over the counter, by mail order and by house calls by salespersons who are salaried employees of the direct writing companies. Many of these companies are owned by conglomerates.

Theoretically, direct selling such as this is supposed to cut the cost of insurance to the consumer by "eliminating the middleman." But in practice most direct selling has not slashed the cost at all and many of the direct writing companies give the public very inferior service.

Much of the property/casualty business in the United States presently is in a mess because of the pernicious and unintelligent policies of some of the bigger direct writing companies. In spite of the huge sales of these companies and their vast outlays on advertising, their actual operation has, in the eyes of many sound professional insurance people, turned out to be a stultifying failure with disastrous consequences for the public. Their vaunted mass merchandising methods have not reduced the cost of automobile, fire and other property/casualty insurance to the American people. On the contrary, they have contributed by their programs and their bad management to runaway increases in costs. They constantly give their customers and other claimants a hard time and force too many claimants to sue in the courts, thus jamming our court calendars and inflating costs by piling up large and unnecessary legal fees. Their widely trumpeted claims to provide fast, fair and comprehensive service to motorists and homeowners are obviously false. Their services actually are stingy and pathetically slow compared with those provided by agents and the companies that market through agents.

There are many reasons for this colossal failure, but the all-important one is that they depend on ill-trained salaried employees instead of independent professionals to carry out every phase of their business. The salaried insurance worker on comparatively modest pay simply does not have the kind of incentive and professional interest in building a personal clientele that the independent agent has. He or she has no more interest in careful and conscientious attention to details in order to build for the future than a girl selling toothpaste in Woolworth's. The policyholder never can be more to such an employee than a name typed at the top of a computer printout form.

On the other hand, the insurance agent is a kind of entrepreneur and that's the kind of person it takes to conduct either property/casualty or life insurance selling and services properly.

The modern agent who has seen the light no longer pushes whole life cash value life insurance on his clients to excess or even at all. He devotes his main effort in life insurance to term protection in adequate amounts at vastly cheaper premium rates.

To get back to using your own efforts and some expert help to program your savings and investing, your chances of success are excellent if you work hard at it and are patient and conservative. Of course, there will be some setbacks. Stocks and bonds go down as well as up; so do interest rates, and recessions can slash corporate earnings and reduce some of your dividends. But if you are patient, the yield on your savings and investments will be compounded in the long run because the economy of the United States still is the greatest in the world and still is growing. But if you are impatient, you are pretty sure to make serious mistakes and be confounded by losses.

Even if your modest saving and investment program is quite successful, it will not provide adequate financial protection for your family if you die early. Even a profitable business or professional practice is not likely to do that. Such a business or practice takes in a lot of money, but it has a high overhead cost and may involve substantial rather illiquid capital investments. The success of a professional practice depends entirely on the skills and personality of the principal, and many an ordinary commercial business may be similarly so dependent on the talents of the proprietor that it is not readily salable. Even if the business can be sold, the family might not get much immediate cash out of it.

So you will need substantial term life insurance protection during your prime years, just as a man or woman with dependents who works for a salary does.

That brings us back to the sham of the universal life policy. Many companies will try to sell you this policy instead of sensible term insurance that provides maximum protection for minimum premium. They will tell you it bridges the gap between term and whole life and incorporates the good features of both.

If you think that sounds impossible on the face of it, you're 100 percent correct.

The companies marketing universal life say it accomplishes the seemingly impossible by being very flexible, giving the policyholder the right to alter the face value of the policy, the premium rate and some other terms to fit the changing protection needs of the family.

So what's new about that? It has always been possible to cancel one life insurance policy and buy another if one's protection needs changed.

The truth is, thus, that the universal life policy is a hoax, a sham cosmetic job on the traditional whole life cash value policy. It is a desperation tactic designed to keep the business locked in the hands of the establishment companies and to retain as much as possible of the excessively high profits these companies have enjoyed for a hundred and fifty years. Of course the profit margins have been slashed somewhat in recent years by the vigorous competition of term insurance, but they are still quite cushy.

Like many other overpriced policies, universal life is sold partly by appealing to the customers' vanity, making it appear that possession of a universal life policy adds significantly to one's status. This is done by endowing universal life with a mystique. The mystique is one of the oldest weapons of the con man and the sharp business operator. It also is employed in politics, education, health care, literature and other arts and, of course, in the more esoteric areas of philosophy and religion. It is based on the idea that if something is difficult or impossible to comprehend, it must be important and highly desirable.

Well, when they got down to actually writing the policies, the companies selling universal life made them impossible to understand. The policies were put together hastily and loaded with gimmicks thought up by the ad men and sales managers until even the executives and actuaries of the companies could not understand them. Some financial journalists who cover the insurance industry also say they found the press release describing the new universal life policies incomprehensible and their claims difficult to accept, to say the least. These journalists are not insurance experts, but they know the basics of life insurance and of economics, and it appears that they couldn't make the claims for the universal policy square with either.

If the insurance company executives and actuaries can't understand these policies, neither can the agents in the field. The universal policy got off to a good sales start because of its novelty and partly because of the mystique, but how in the world can the sales forces in these companies continue to sell the policies over the long haul if they don't understand the product and can't describe and explain it to customers?

Pretty soon, the public is going to wake up and realize that the mystique and the policies add up just to a big hoax and the policies are not what the companies claim they are. These companies won't be able to delude today's customers the way they deluded people in the past into buying vastly overpriced and grossly inadequate protection.

The fact that a sham like the universal life policy has enjoyed such an initial success is further evidence that a large number of Americans rob themselves or allow themselves to be robbed by remaining uninformed about elemental economics and business principles. It is disgraceful that this goes on in a country where information is so freely obtainable if you look for it.

Part of the fault is the breakdown of discipline in our schools, too many unruly kids being passed up through the grades without actually learning much. There also has been a breakdown of discipline in the teaching profession, so we have in the grade schools a number of teachers who don't know the subjects they are supposed to be teaching. They hold their jobs by pull and various pressure manipulations. But this is by no means the major cause of the evil. Nor are con men or the criminally sharp business operators the biggest exploiters of the uninformed. The worst perpetrators are the guardians of the status quo, the people who stick their heads in the sand like the ostrich and pretend things always will stay as they are, and those privileged characters in society who have a selfish and ruthlessly maintained interest in preventing the generality of mankind from looking ahead intelligently.

These are the establishment people who rule business and politics and build up vast collective and individual empires founded on entrenched and profitable privileges. Preserving these privileges often involves the exercise of tyrannical power and much hypocrisy. It also may depend on preserving obsolescence and economic folly.

To accomplish their ends, these privileged few like to keep the rest of us in the dark, unable to see the truth until it is too late.

These privileged few are not part of our

acknowledged criminal element. On the contrary, they are mainly those smugly respectable persons sometimes referred to as the "Pillars of Society." In their forefront quite naturally are found the inside stockholder and management oligarchies of establishment life insurance companies.

Although it seems otherwise to the great majority of us who are destined never to enter the ranks of the privileged few, their struggle to maintain the status quo always ends in failure, because the law of life is change and the pace of social and economic change has accelerated greatly in this century and is now moving along even faster. The reason so many of us fail to realize this is because the changes bring forth new privileged groups to replace those that have fallen by the wayside, and some of the older privileged groups and individuals manage to acquire new privileges to replace those they have lost.

We all know about the rapid turnover of people caused by the almost meteoric changes in those businesses that depend on physical science and technology— agriculture, oil, mining, steel, automobiles, aircraft, chemicals, weapons, electronics and broadcasting of entertainment and information, for example—but change is every bit as rapid, perhaps more so, in such prosaic businesses as retailing, wholesaling, stock brokerage, real estate, investment management and counselling and insurance.

And now the small personal computer is forcing tremendous procedural changes and enlarging the horizons of executives and even ordinary semi-skilled workers in most departments of all kinds of companies.

Sometimes the changes are seemingly contradictory.

We have seen the Mom 'n' Pop retail store replaced by chain stores, the growth of franchised merchandising, the replacement of many traditional department stores by discount stores. Yet, paradoxically, these developments have not diminished the desire of Americans to go into business for themselves. This desire is so widespread that a whole tribe of new management consultants has sprung up specializing in helping people get into business for themselves.

One such firm in New York made a rather in-depth study of the matter and concluded that about one-third of all those persons in America with a little executive experience who change their careers in the course of an average year still go into business for themselves, and so do many persons who have no previous managerial experience.

The most important reason given for starting one's own business was the transformation of our nation from an industrial society to an economy largely based on service and communications enterprises that, while not labor intensive, do not require very large capital investments.

Also, the fact that the United States now is seen more as part of a global economy than a self-contained national economy has caused many persons, particularly those with roots or associations abroad, to want to go into business for themselves and take advantage of widening markets.

The aging of the population makes some retired persons or persons nearing retirement think about starting a new business. The acquisition of marketable high technology skills by large numbers of individuals is another reason. Why work for someone else if you can market your skills directly at better prices and be independent?

It may seem astounding that the public has let the frightful abuse of whole life cash value insurance go on so long. We have seen how there have been outcries against it on both sides of the Atlantic for a century. *Why didn't the public respond and put a stop to the racket?*

In the first place, the early protests were heard by very few people. They were made in books, and in the nineteenth century a thousand copies was a big printing for a serious book and the readers of such a book were likely to be literary folk rather than serious potential buyers of life insurance.

Attempts to do anything about the abuses in the British Parliament or in the U.S. Congress or state legislatures could be easily stifled by the insurance company lobbyists.

There was another important reason why nothing happened to improve things. Man is a gullible creature. P.T. Barnum wasn't being very original or exaggerating when he said a sucker is born every minute. The reason so many persons live out their lives as suckers is that they find it easier to live with illusions than to knuckle down to the hard task of discovering the truth and facing up to it.

Even unpleasant illusions are cherished; that's why so many persons revel in superstitious belief in demons and witchcraft. A pleasant illusion can really be comforting.

If people thought about life insurance favorably in the nineteenth century they were pretty certain to think of it in the illusory terms the companies desired them to. If they thought about it unfavorably, they rejected it altogether. They weren't concerned about reforming it. Actually life insurance had a generally poor reputation then on both sides of the Atlantic. Most people shunned it, if for no other reason than that it distressed them to even think about the prospect of their own deaths. Sudden death in the prime of life was an ever-present possibility in those days.

Persons who were attracted to buying life insurance had, for the most part, very limited aims. A policy big enough to pay terminal medical bills and funeral expenses and leave a little cash over was all that most thought they could afford. They did not think about life insurance as a means of financial security. Family security then depended on various social entitlements—an inherited place on the land, a pension or patronage benefit, or, most of all, on the right of parents to expect their children to take care of them in their old age. We have seen in this book that, in this country, life insurance's reputation worsened until Charles Evans Hughes led the New York legislature to force the industry to clean up the outright criminal practices in 1905.

After that, the industry enjoyed a remarkable boom that made huge fortunes for life insurance company owners and managements. Its market grew like wildfire because the nation was growing fast and social and economic changes were moving people off the land and weakening family ties, thus creating a need for a new source of security. Improving health standards reduced the fear of untimely death and made people more willing to think about providing for death's consequences. No longer did wives say, "I don't want to think about it!" if their husbands suggested buying a life insurance policy.

Americans of the first quarter of this century worshipped success even more than we do today, and life insurance's success story was as big and dramatic as those of the automobile and oil industries. The establishment companies acquired tremendous social prestige. They also acquired enormous economic power because their huge cash inflow gave them the assets to rival the banks as the providers of mortgage money, construction loans, and all kinds of large-scale investments. Communities all across the land and many industries began to depend on life insurance companies for capital.

Naturally, this accumulated economic power gave the life insurance establishment great political power and it used that power, organizing sophisticated lobbies in all state legislatures, seeking to influence and even control the state insurance regulatory departments.

The great life insurance boom and the acquisition of so much power enabled the establishment companies to create a grand illusion, a super myth that began almost to take on the trappings of a religion. The myth was that whole life cash value insurance was the key to salvation of man here on Earth.

The myth is still believed in by many of the one hundred and fifty million Americans who are locked into overpriced inadequate insurance policies, and it is difficult to destroy the myth unless people can be induced to think about it seriously and rationally.

The great boom for the establishment companies continued through the middle of the 1960's and in the latter part of the whole period several things happened that fortified and magnified the myth. One was the development of group life insurance paid for out of payroll deductions or more frequently paid for outright by employers. This provided many times as much protection at much cheaper rates than the old-fashioned industrial insurance paid for at fifty to sixty cents a week, paid to a collector who came to the plant regularly. The rise of group life greatly enhanced the image of the life insurance industry in general.

So did the rapid growth of health insurance, although the establishment companies didn't have much to do with creating popular health insurance. But they got on the bandwagon and basked in the improved public and social image of life insurance that health insurance created.

But when they invented Key Man and other jumbo business life policies, the image of the establishment companies really began to take on lustre. Not only was this business very profitable, it was glamorous and dramatic. Life insurance policies were elevated to be important strategic tools of corporations and partnerships, and such a jumbo policy became a gilded status symbol for a financial or industrial tycoon.

In spite of the abuses and the gross inadequacy of the protection, life insurance was giving millions of persons benefits their forebears had never dreamed of enjoying. And the business was so profitable it was making comfortable livings for many men and women all across the country who did not realize they were selling their customers inferior products. They had been brainwashed, as I was when I first entered the business. But gradually the number of dissenters increased and subtly and slowly the bright image of the myth began to fade and tarnish.

Many of the dissenters did much more than protest. They founded new companies to sell term insurance, providing vastly more protection in the prime years at much lower premiums. Individual term life began to catch on with the better informed element of the public. Thinking people asked for it and many agents began to think it might be the wave of the future.

I have already told how the establishment companies fought back and how their lobbyists utilized their influence on the state regulatory authorities to block agents from helping customers to switch from whole life cash value insurance to term. The volume of brand new term life sold began to become impressive in the 1960's. Even the establishment companies were forced grudgingly to sell individual term insurance if customers demanded it.

But it wasn't until around the end of the 1970's that the new pure term life companies began to find ways to make a massive sales attack on the overpriced, inadequate policies many Americans had been paying on for so many years.

Inflation gave poignant incentive to the task. If a man died in these years leaving a wife and three children and a $25,000 life insurance policy, the widow had to face the bitter fact that her husband had left only half as much as he intended when he bought the policy. Inflation had cut its buying power in half.

The agents had to bear the brunt of the tarnishing of the bright myth. Many were not able to increase their sales and they could not answer much of the criticism of their policies they were getting from customers.

And it was from agents that the way to attack the main problem came. They realized that it was a marketing task, and that relatively small new insurance companies couldn't possibly match the widespread marketing facilities of the big establishment companies. But some far-seeing agents realized that they could develop marketing strategies and recruit sales forces big enough to do the job, and they set to work at it. Not surprisingly, the earliest efforts in this direction were too tentative and too limited in scope. Nevertheless, they were sufficiently successful to demonstrate that the principles followed were sound. They only needed refinement and more rigorous and vigorous application. That is now being done.

In spite of the recent successes of companies selling

combinations of term life insurance and annuities or mutual funds, I think it will be necessary to get some federal regulation of the insurance industry if the octopus really is to be vanquished. Perhaps the defeat in the 1982 elections of Senator Howard Cannon of Nevada will make that easier. He was the man who persuaded Congress to hamstring the Federal Trade Commission's plans to investigate the business further following its dramatic 1979 report.

In addition to all the other reasons given in Chapters 2 and 3 for favoring repeal of the McCarran-Ferguson Act in order to permit federal regulation, I have been struck in the past three years by the mounting cost burden of regulation of the insurance business by fifty separate state authorities. I now am convinced that this excessively high regulatory cost is a major factor in keeping the price of both life insurance and property/casualty (including automobile) insurance to the public much higher than it ought to be.

The many ways by which Americans rob themselves or allow themselves to be robbed all more or less amount to the same thing as making "sucker bets" on football games or while playing at cards or dice. A sucker bet is one made at unfairly short odds; if you win, you don't get anywhere near as much as you should, while the chap offering the short odds wins most of his bets and isn't out much on the few he loses.

People make sucker bets because they don't know the correct odds. They haven't studied the game or the proposition they are betting on carefully enough.

Gambling isn't nowadays considered a respectable way of making a living, but that hasn't always been the case. In some eras very successful gamblers were greatly admired. Perhaps that was because people felt instinctively that there is an inevitable element of chance in almost every human activity and therefore the gambler was a romantic figure and a man of mystery because no one really knew what made him succeed. His triumphs were often attributed to sheer physical endurance and audacity, to ice-cold nerves or to a mesmeric ability to intimidate his opponents into giving up or making serious mistakes.

Doubtless the ice-cold nerves, physical endurance and daring are essential to the good gambler, but the real secret of his success is much more prosaic—he knows the correct odds and those whom he vanquishes and takes money from do not. He never makes a bet unless the odds are right, and he lures his opponents into making one sucker bet after another.

It follows that an exceptional feeling for mathematics and the resulting ability to precisely analyze odds quickly on any given hazard are what make the successful gambler.

The most famous gambler of all time was John Law (1671–1729), the Scot who later came acropper by persuading the French monarchy to indulge in the spectacularly inflationary Mississippi Bubble.* Law won many millions of pounds in European gambling halls because he was the only man in Europe with the mathematical skill to calculate the correct odds in every kind of game of chance.

A life insurance policy is a wager against death by the insurance company, and for a hundred and fifty years the establishment companies have lured Americans into

___
*See Arthur Milton, *Inflation: Everybody's Problem* (Secaucus, N.J.: Citadel Press. 1968).

making sucker bets on the matter at extremely short and unfair odds. It works this way:

By writing a policy on a person's whole life, the company, in theory, faces the certainty of losing its wager, since we all must die, but we have seen in this book that really isn't true (the certainty of the loss of the wager, that is). Nevertheless, the assumption allows the company an excuse to give the policyholder only extremely short odds in the wager.

On the other hand, the companies can and do offer the customers much longer odds when they buy term life insurance because, obviously, the shorter the term of the policy the greater the chance that the policyholder will not die while it is in force. So the customer gets a lower premium rate and long odds.

Buying a whole life cash value policy thus is like making an even money bet on a football game when the bookies actually are offering good odds against the team you want to bet on. Or it can be like being switched into betting on the wrong game. The customer thinks he is betting on financial protection against early death when, in fact, the company has switched him into a bet on ultimate death.

Even if you don't buy overpriced whole life insurance, you are robbing yourself if you are in your prime years and do not buy adequate term life protection for your wife and children. If you do not, you are making a sucker bet that your savings, investments, group insurance and perhaps your business will yield an adequate amount of cash for their needs. The odds you are giving yourself and your family on that proposition are very short indeed, whereas a good, adequate term life policy would give you long odds protection against early death.

Many persons will rob themselves by not setting up tax-deferred annuities, an IRA, Keogh Plan or a mutual fund for their later years. If you fail to do this, you will pay out unnecessary sums in income taxes that you and your family could enjoy later in life.

If you have money left over for investment and squander it away instead of buying a good mutual fund, you are again robbing yourself.

You are robbing your family if you do not build up an estate from savings and investments because when you are in your sixties and seventies the cost of financial protection by means of whole life insurance will be grossly inadequate.

But perhaps the most important way Americans rob themselves is by general neglect—not spending the time and effort to keep up reasonably well with the changing social and economic scene, not knowing anything about the different kinds of annuities and savings accounts available, about tax-exempt municipal securities, about the various kinds of mutual funds or about the stock market.

You may be robbing yourself if you fail to get expert advice in buying term insurance. The price can vary quite a bit from company to company, and there are many kinds of term insurance. Just how much you need and what type of policy will depend on your age, your present income, the ages of your children and what your family's goals are for the years immediately ahead. The state of your health is a factor, too, since you want to remain insurable as long as your dependents need the protection. If you also have elderly parents or siblings dependent on you, this raises a separate protection problem to be solved. A mistake could have costly and devastating consequences.

I have attempted in this chapter to motivate you to act now to improve your long-term financial position as well as to provide financial security for your loved ones.

The responsibility rests with you to have a firm foundation first and then build upon it for your House of Financial Independence.

14. *The Heart of the Matter*

Combining term insurance and assorted other investments . . . The agent as a money doctor . . . Varieties and costs of term life insurance.

I CAN SAY WITHOUT HESITATION that no two people think alike, no two people earn income exactly alike, and certainly no two people spend their money alike. The insurance business has fallen down horribly by not training its extensive sales organizations to advise people on the broad matter of money as it pertains to all individuals.

Now I must come to the big question—what should people in the prime of life do about creating an immediate estate by insurance and an ultimate estate by saving and investing?

Obviously, the second half of my question requires more definitive answers far beyond the scope of this book, but I can point you to a sound start at achieving a satisfactory answer.

In simplest terms, the couple should create an immediate estate by means of term life insurance and plan for an ultimate estate by means of tax-deferred annuities, mutual funds, savings bank accounts, and perhaps investments in stocks and bonds and real estate. The best way for the average person to get involved in the great progress that our country will enjoy throughout the 1990's right into the 21st century is by way of a well-managed mutual fund.

Tailor-making your present and future financial security should not be taken lightly. Honesty between you and your advisor or advisors is of paramount importance. By that I mean don't get mixed up with a professional advisor who thinks commission dollars first and you second. On the other hand, you, too, must be honest. There is no point in telling your advisor about money problems that don't exist now or may never exist. For example, if you have the ability to set aside fifteen hundred dollars a year for your financial security and that of your family in the event of your premature death, don't tell the money doctor that the figure is three times that amount. He or she will only come back to you with an elaborate plan that you can't possibly put into effect. The whole program ends up in the wastepaper basket and you and your family walk around naked, without proper financial security.

Financial planning for the average person can be very simple. If there is a need for life insurance, buy term (the cheapest) and invest the difference. One really doesn't need a Wharton School graduate for this advice. You need a Proper Honest Director whose philosophy agrees with your requirements.

To put things in the right order, let us consider term

insurance needs first. How much and what kind does the average couple need?

As an ideal minimum, most experts think a couple with one child should have $200,000 worth of term insurance during the prime years, $300,000 for two children, and an extra $50,000 for each additional child. Admittedly, a lot of people can afford the premiums for $200,000–$300,000 worth of term coverage and meet their other obligations, too.

There are many kinds of term insurance, but only a few need be discussed.

Group term is the kind of insurance your employer buys for you. If you have some of it, you naturally take that into consideration when buying other coverage. But the amount of an individual's group life insurance is generally not enough to satisfy family needs for death insurance, and, as a rule, you lose it if you change employers.

Annual renewable term: the face amount of the policy is payable upon the death of the insured during the period for which the premium has been paid. The policy expires after one year unless renewed each year by the policyholder paying a revised annual premium, which is slightly higher in each succeeding year. A word of caution—always make sure that the policy you are buying gives you the privilege of renewing and converting without further medical examination. Your good health today, unfortunately, may not assure your total insurability at all or at standard rates tomorrow. Renewable term can also be purchased for periods other than one year, such as a five-year renewable-convertible term policy. Depending on the age at issue, the average premium over the years can be more or less than that of the yearly renewable term.

Level premium term: Some companies have worked out a level premium term policy for periods of ten, fifteen or twenty years. These are ideal contracts, particularly for the young family in which it will take that period of time for the children to grow and be on their own. For example, the age thirty-five breadwinner would be well advised to buy a twenty-year level term product, making sure that assets in other areas were built upon so that by the time he or she is age fifty-five to sixty-five, the need for death insurance need not exist.

Decreasing term can be the least expensive in premium cost. The reason is obvious. The face amount of the policy decreases each year and eventually becomes zero at the terminal age of the policy. Probably the best application for decreasing term insurance is to cover a business or home mortgage where the indebtedness declines each year and so your insurance may be permitted to decline.

One thing to make sure of is that you choose term insurance that is guaranteed to be renewable and convertible without further medical examination.

Quality discounts are now prevalent in buying term insurance. Comparing the real cost and relative merits of five-year renewable term insurance, level term, and diminishing term is not easy. (As I've indicated previously, competition within the industry dictates that you get the best possible honest advice.) Before inflation became so acute, many persons considered diminishing term the best. Obviously, it is cheaper in the long run than five-year renewable term with the death benefit kept level at the maximum figure.

But inflation introduced a new element into the picture. During the earlier and middle period of life, inflation makes it incumbent on many couples to increase their insurance protection year by year instead of letting it slowly decrease. This makes a straight term policy more attractive than the diminishing policy. Actually, few buyers of five-year renewable keep the death benefit level. They raise or lower it each renewal according to changes in their protection needs, raising and lowering the premiums accordingly. If an increase is desirable, you had better make sure you maintain your health to be insurable. That is why I always recommend a big chunk of term insurance early, preferably a level premium for twenty years. It is cheap enough and can protect your future insurability.

Since term life insurance is neither a savings nor an investment instrument but is only protection for survivors in case of untimely death, those who rely on it must make sensible savings and investment plans early. The inflationary climate of the 1970's and 1980's has changed both savings and investment pictures. For example, bank accounts, which used to pay very low interest rates even though the interest was compounded, now pay a much more reasonable return on some types of savings certificates.

Certificates of deposits in banks have become very popular and provide even the small saver with excellent interest-income returns. These certificates can be purchased for as short a period as six months.

Gold and silver, paintings, fine ceramics, antiques, postage stamps, and a variety of other art objects that investment counselors can call "collectibles" have grown enormously in value because of inflation, and the critical international political situation at the start of 1980 has accelerated this trend. Who would have expected to see gold hit $835 an ounce while the official U.S. mint price still is only about $40.00? Or the almost nine hundred percent rise in the price of silver in a year? But any collectible can be highly speculative. With inflation down considerably since 1980, most of the odd-ball, hare-brained collectibles have diminished in value tremendously. Gold prices are now under $400 per ounce as compared to $835 at their high in 1980.

Real estate, of course, has climbed out of sight because of inflation and because so many people need homes. Even some of the real estate investment trusts on which stockholders and banks lost billions of dollars in the early 1970's are starting to come back.

Although the progression of value in real estate has generally been true, I have seen countless persons lose their shirts in attempting to invest in this complicated field. Part-time venturers buy at the wrong time, only to suffer huge losses when they have to sell. It takes real skill to invest in real estate at any level, whether you are considering raw land, apartment houses, or office buildings. For the average person, the only real estate they should consider is the purchase of their own home.

Tax-exempt municipal bonds have also made something of a comeback, and new tax-exempt issues are paying better yields. I question, however, the advisability of investing in this area. Near financial collapse of so many cities such as New York, Cleveland, and Yonkers has caused me to wonder whether an investment in municipal bonds is prudent. After all, would you invest in any bond in any corporation where you knew the management was inept?

The trouble with all these investments is that, except for bank deposits, where the Federal Deposit Insurance

Corporation insures your account up to a hundred thousand dollars, they require unflagging study of the market trends and great expertise. You have to pick one or two fields and learn them yourself. No financial advisor could hope to keep up with them all.

That leaves the stock market, mutual funds, and annuities.

As for the stock market, there are, indeed, many bargains to be found in it, but one may have to wait a long time to realize the gain. Prices on the New York Stock Exchange are not currently inflated as much as the general economy, so the present is a good time for making long-term investments in good stocks. It is not a good time to try for short-term profits by trading in shares. On the other hand, prices of stocks listed only on some of the minor stock exchanges and in the over-the-counter market are inflated like the general economy, because institutions and private citizens are speculating in these markets. But whether investing or speculating, putting money in stocks takes up an awful lot of time and requires a tremendous amount of expert knowledge these days. What everyone hopes to find in the stock market is a special situation, a company with great growth prospects as yet undiscovered by the securities analysts and the speculators but fairly certain to be discovered soon. A relatively small investment in such a stock can run into a fortune.

But what happens to most investors is that they buy "glamour" stocks after the prices have already been run up, the way the gambling-casino shares skyrocketed in 1978 and early 1979. Then they hang on too long or not long enough and sell when all the rest of the panicky speculators are selling. Periodically, the glamour stocks have to tumble like houses of cards because their prices have run up far more than can be justified by any realistic earnings or expansion potential. Only the astute traders and investors buy and sell at the psychologically right times and make any money out of them.

As another word of caution: There have been too many headline stories of stockbrokers, even those connected with some of the more prestigious Wall Street houses, who took customers and their capital the way Grant took Virginia.

Once again, the greed of much of humanity must be watched carefully, particularly when investing in Wall Street. As mentioned earlier, the churning of funds to constantly earn commissions for the benefit of stockbrokers and to bleed customers is an ongoing problem.

Most Americans should not purchase individual stocks for their financial security. That's why mutual funds become an ideal investment. A mutual fund generally invests in a variety of industries and gives an opportunity for the average American to still create a stake in America's future growth without high risk.

In a *New York Times* article of September 3, 1989, it talks about the "little guys" and how many of them are steering clear of stocks and bonds and investing in mutual funds. Some $250 billion in assets is what the "little guys" own. Do they really need cash value policies to force them to save money? "Humbug!" I say to that old, old propaganda of the life insurance companies. I just have to get more and more of my followers to do the same thing for themselves and their families as these other "little guys."

And so I recommend to you to follow the crowd if you want a stake in an ever-growing country—your country and mine. Buy into one or more well-managed mutual funds with your extra dollars.*

Before going into the virtues of tax-deferred annuities, it may be well to make clear the difference between a tax deferment and a tax shelter. A tax deferment is simply a means of putting off paying taxes for some years. This serves two purposes: It enables an investment to grow faster by reinvesting the interest it earns, and it puts off payment of taxes on the interest until a time when one expects to be in a lower tax bracket than now. Additionally, taxes might come down through the workings of some miraculous reform in Washington. That has happened several times in our national history, although this generation might find that hard to believe, and as late as 1986 tax rates were reduced substantially.

Further changes in taxation methods within the next decade make tax-deferred annuities very, very attractive at this time. The possibility of going from the high-structured income tax system of today to a value-added tax system is real. I predict that Congress will and must do something fast; otherwise the underground economy will become larger and larger and make taxation for the honest people more and more burdensome.

A tax shelter, on the other hand, is a means of avoiding or attempting to avoid taxes on certain income altogether and to create paper losses that can be used to offset taxes on other income. Since many persons who have some money to invest are solicited frequently by promoters of tax shelters, it may be well to say a little about them. Tax shelters are of two kinds, the legitimate and the dubious, and many of the dubious ones are plain attempted fraud. But the promoters still succeed in selling

*See Arthur Milton, *Milton on America* (Secaucus, N.J.: Citadel Press, 1986).

a lot of them and then disappearing, leaving the investors to hold the bag when the IRS cracks down. The dubious shelters are built around all sorts of schemes involving coal mining lands, old motion pictures and master phonograph records for which there is little demand, unsold stocks of newly printed books, fifth-rate paintings and other art objects, and bizarre mining prospects. Some of them involve charity-donation wrinkles.

They all have two common features—grossly inflated valuations of the property or merchandise involved and the creation of large amounts of nonrecourse debt, which the investor is told to take as a deduction against his or her other taxable income so as to get down into a much lower tax bracket. Nonrecourse debt is money the debtor owes on paper but is not really obligated to pay—the creditor has no legal recourse. Because the IRS takes a very jaundiced look at all deductions based on nonrecourse debt, the tax-shelter promoters try to disguise it as genuine "at risk" debt. The IRS is probably never really fooled by this, but a lot of tax returns with such deductions do get by, just by escaping being audited. When a taxpayer is caught at this kind of shenanigan, Uncle Sam can be quite nasty about it. Nineteen eighty-four saw a drastic change in the Internal Revenue Service's attitudes toward many tax shelter gimmicks. New rules are being applied to curb tax shelter abuses.

Legitimate tax shelters are those authorized by Congress for specific purposes, such as to encourage housing construction or exploration and drilling for oil and gas. Direct or participation investment in these activities can create unrealized losses that can be used to shelter other income from taxes. But investors must be very careful in purchasing participations in these activities, legitimate as they are. A number of them have been marketed by fast-buck artists who structured them with a grossly unfair division of profit and risk. The promoters skim off most of the potential profit in advance, and the investor is left with a small amount of profit and big risks. There are a lot of good legitimate real estate and petroleum tax-sheltered participations, but you must know how to find reputable dealers and operators, and investing in them usually takes quite a chunk of capital.

Annuities have been sold all over the world for many years by life insurance companies, but in the United States they have not been pushed hard simply because a life insurance agent may make a much better commission by selling a whole life cash value insurance policy with the same premium.

Annuities pay much better yields than cash value insurance for a variety of reasons, and their tax-deferment feature is a great help to many persons. Annuities come in several types, according to both the way one pays money into them and the way the annuitant gets it back with interest.

There are single-premium annuities on which the investor pays in a substantial lump sum either all at once or in two or three installments and then draws monthly payments from the fund and its accumulated earnings, starting either fairly soon or on retirement.

Then there is the flexible or installment annuity, to which the investor makes monthly or quarterly deposits over a period of years until the full amount has been paid.

Now, let's look at annuities in accordance with the way the money comes back to you.

The life-only option. The company guarantees to pay you a fixed monthly income, from the time agreed for payments to start until you die. But if you die after receiving only a few payments your widow and dependents get nothing. It's not a good plan, needless to say, and I don't recommend this option. It is weighted too much in favor of the insurance company.

Installment-refund option: Provides a refund to your beneficiary if you die before receiving enough payments to equal the deposits you have paid in plus the accumulated interest. I recommend this option.

Life and ten or twenty years certain: If you die soon after starting to receive payments, the company will continue payments to your widow or beneficiary for the remainder of an agreed ten or twenty year period, but if you outlive this agreed period you continue to get payments for the rest of your life.

Joint and survivor option: Once they start, the monthly income payments are made during the lifetimes of two persons, usually husband and wife. Under some plans, however, the payments to the survivor may be smaller than the payments made while both are living.

Regardless of the plan chosen, annuities have certain important benefit characteristics:

• The money you pay in comes out of your taxed income or your capital, hence can never again be subject to income tax. Only the interest it subsequently earns can be taxed.

• Taxes on this interest are deferred until the money comes back to you in the shape of monthly income payments or in a lump sum.

• If your contract designates someone other than yourself as annuitant when it is purchased, then no income tax is payable if you die before the period of return payments begins.

• An annuity account can be transferred from one life insurance company to another without incurring any tax obligation on the interest funds. But such a transfer must be arranged by the new company or its agent. If you withdraw the funds yourself, even with the intent of buying a new annuity, the interest immediately becomes taxable. The right procedure is known as a "roll-over."

As with life insurance policies, there is an enormous variation in the prices insurance companies charge for similar annuities and there are huge differences in their terms and quality. Beware the hard sell annuity pitch. The front-end-loaded tax deferred annuities being sold by many insurance companies often have tremendous discrepancies between the promises in the sales pitches and the funds' actual performance.

No financially sophisticated person would buy a front-end-loaded annuity. Many responsible companies now market a new kind of no-load single-premium deferred annuity. Interest is paid on 100 percent of the principal from the date of issue of the policy. There are no off-the-top reductions for commissions or overhead. The company guarantees to return the entire principal at any time under most circumstances. The interest rate is generally guaranteed for one year from issue, and an interest rate of at least four percent is guaranteed no matter how bad business conditions get.

In August 1982, the ballgame changed for new buyers of single premium deferred annuities. The Tax Equity Fiscal Responsibility Act, also commonly known as TEFRA, came into being and the provisions concerning the withdrawal of funds from the annuity account were revised from their previous position. Now, all withdrawals from the annuity account are considered withdrawals of interest first, and are therefore taxable in the year received. In addition, there is a federally-imposed five percent excise tax if the funds are withdrawn before you attain age 59½.

The return-payment options are similar to those already described. The company is able to avoid charging big front-end fees because it is willing to wait years to reap its profit. Meanwhile, it absorbs the sales commissions and other costs gradually out of the margin between the interest it pays on the annuity funds and what it earns on them.

It is certain that the tax-deferred annuity with a relatively high-interest yield is the best and perhaps the only way many persons can be sure of offsetting inflation and providing a retirement income to supplement Social Security.

I like to call annuities a place to put your real serious money so that, come the twilight years, you will not be held holding the bag with nothing but your meagre Social Security benefits.

When the advantages of current-day annuities are measured—
—1. principle guarantee
—2. liquidity of your money
—3. guaranteed interest return
—4. compounding of interest
—5. taxes at payout only
—6. income payment designated at and when needed
—7. estate and death and probate advantages

I ask any legitimate professional in the life insurance industry, "Who needs cash value life insurance in any form?" "Nobody," can be their only honest answer. And they will sell you the concept of "buy term and invest the difference" if they have *your* interests at heart.

If ever a guaranteed investment was designed to take advantage of the miracle of compound interest, annuities are it.

A couple may accumulate an ultimate estate by hard work, intelligence, and good fortune over a reasonably long lifespan, but untimely death means that the immediate estate becomes the ultimate estate.

But remember, persons in the prime of life won't be drawing annuity-income payments for many years. Nor will they enjoy the benefit of their well-managed mutual fund investment right away. In the meantime, they need death insurance, lots of it at reasonable prices, and it's time to compel all life insurance companies to provide it and nothing but it.

A lifetime of hard work should result in hard assets to fall back on—*and always remember how hard you work for your money so that it can one day work hard for you.*

15. *Tell Yesterday Goodbye*

The results of the life insurance industry's greed and ignorance . . . Can the industry reform itself? Will they? . . . The problems of yesterday and hopes for tomorrow.

A NINETEENTH CENTURY philosopher said the trouble with life is that we have to look at it backwards to understand it, but we must live it by looking ahead.

Most persons instinctively try to order their lives by looking forward but, sadly, many of us are like a fellow riding backwards in a passenger train: we never see anything until it has passed us by. Consequently many of our enterprises and our careers become casualties in the continual struggle for progress.

Moreover, society contains a lot of characters who have a selfish and ruthlessly maintained interest in preventing us from looking ahead intelligently. These are the establishment people who rule business and politics and build up vast collective and individual empires founded on entrenched and profitable privilege.

This profitable privilege for the few at the expense of the many is based quite simply on greed and ignorance and it depends on the exercise of tyrannical power and on cynical chicanery and hypocrisy. Preserving the privilege often depends on preserving and protecting obsolescence and economic folly.

Chairman Walter B. Wriston of New York's Citicorp told the insurance forum on November 18, 1982, that these guardians of the status quo have a special scorn for people who articulate new ideas. *Wriston also pointed out that "one can predict with confidence that, in the great American tradition, the first thing industry does when faced with competition is yell for protection."*

Often, this protection is forthcoming, so big business and even little business and their lawyers succeed in maintaining privilege and slowing down the march of progress. But not forever and often not for long. After reciting a long list of changes in the insurance and other financial service industries that increased competition, Wriston said, "looking backward teaches us that the velocity of change has not slowed down, even though each trade association will make a generation of lawyers rich and clog our court system in vain attempts to preserve yesterday."

And, in the context of this book, who is striving the hardest to preserve yesterday?

The established life insurance companies, naturally.

Having enjoyed a license to steal for a hundred and fifty years, they are trying desperately to cling to the privileged position that they have used to bamboozle the American people out of many billions of dollars by selling them grossly inadequate death insurance protection at absurdly high prices on the specious pretexts that buying life insurance is a good way to save money, there can be such a thing as permanent insurance, and that most people need it.

Although the false claims for their endowment policies, limited payment policies and whole life, cash value insurance were thoroughly exploded twenty years ago by the proponents of sensibly priced term death insurance in amounts adequate to protect a family during its prime years, these fatcat companies have by no means given up the struggle to keep their power and their ill-gotten fat profits.

In an August 21, 1989, cover story article, *Business Week* magazine gave some insights that explain why the established industry continues to hang on. "As a legal cartel, it reaped bountiful profits and came to control enormous assets, now more than $1.8 trillion. It's premium income is 9% of the GNP. Few industries have ever enjoyed such unchecked political and economic power." No wonder industry fatcats are eager to hang on to yesterday!

As I discussed earlier, the latest device for achieving this is, a gimmick called the "universal life" insurance policy, which nobody can understand and which does nothing to provide adequate protection against the financial consequences of premature death at reasonable premium rates.

I declare flatly that all the so-called universal life insurance policies are nothing more than another sham to replace the cash value, whole life policies that have become, oh, so obsolete. Their introduction and promotion in the past few years makes it obvious that the establishment companies are determined to preserve all the evils of yesterday they can.

But they will not succeed in doing so, even though the gimmicky universal policies got off to a fairly good sales start initially. You can't fool the public for long; soon they'll wake up and realize that these policies are not what the companies claim they are. The blunt truth is that they are so hastily put together and so gimmicky that not even the executives and the actuaries of the companies understand them. So how in the world can the sales forces of these companies keep on successfully selling a product they don't understand and cannot describe and explain to the customers? They won't be able to delude today's customers the way people were deluded in the past. Today's increasingly educated and informed consumer has too much saavy to continue to allow giant whole life companies to bilk them of thousands of dollars of their hard-earned income. Times are changing, people are changing, and it's time for business giants who continue to promote obsolete products that are not in the best interest of consumers to change with those times—if they want to survive. The good old days are gone; and actually, the good old days weren't so good. In many ways they were awful.

Life insurance wasn't the only business whose practitioners acted as if they had a license to steal. Even more flagrant was the larceny of those licensed to trade in stocks and bonds in Wall Street on behalf of members of the investing public, who usually were referred to as "the lambs," meaning those whose function was to be fleeced.

Being a stockbroker was a cushy thing in those days. Many of the brokers sailed to work each day down the Hudson or East River in their palatial private yachts and moored them at the public docks. A young Princeton graduate named Fred Schwed, Jr., who worked briefly in Wall Street aroused a lot of chuckles when he wrote a little book about his experiences and entitled it, "Where Are the Customers' Yachts?"

One of the biggest requirements of the job was to have an elastic conscience. One could not be above a little judicious and profitable churning of the accounts of rich relatives and friends. Churning, of course, means engaging in trades just for the sake of generating commissions. Hopefully, the customers wouldn't actually lose more than the amount of the commissions, but that was far from always the case. Even today, some of the biggest and most prominent Wall Street houses have been sued for very large sums as a result of unconscionable churning of customers' portfolios and countless other unethical practices. (You only have to pick up a newspaper to witness the continuing saga of abuses in the securities industry).

At that time, investments in securities were almost exclusively the province of the wealthy. Mutual funds were the first effort to make stocks and bonds affordable investments for little people. Invented way back in the early 1930's, mutual funds grew like wildfire in the late 1950's and 1960's and are still flourishing.

Then, a few years ago, along came the discount brokerage house, which eliminated the high cost of individually handled accounts and put the buying and selling of securities on much the same basis as buying apples in a grocery store or nuts and bolts in a hardware shop. This slashed the commissions people had to pay to buy or sell stocks and bonds or commodities futures up to, in some instances, as much as 75 percent.

The discount brokerage house was a logical development for other and possibly more important reasons than the elimination of the "license to steal" of the irresponsible old-fashioned brokers. It sprang up as a natural result of certain trends. One such trend was the development of a large number of independent financial planning and investment counselors not affiliated with bank trust departments or the securities industry who began to offer their services to the public. Some of these persons called themselves "money doctors" and advertised that they could look after the financial health of a family the way a medical general practitioner looks after the family's physical health. The actual knowledge and capabilities of these new independent financial planners and counselors varied tremendously, but most of them had either good academic credentials or fairly good track records of performance in various financial service fields. They were much better educated and trained on the whole than brokerage house registered representatives.

The largest single block of these new financial planners are now found in insurance.

A second trend is increased consumer awareness in the last 20 years. An increasing proportion of the people in America with money to invest are far better educated and far more knowledgeable than in the past. Nowadays many persons in the investing public have attended college, had a course or two in economics, basic accounting and the elements of business management. They have learned how to read the financial section of the newspaper intelligently, listen to business news on the air, and lots of them read the *Wall Street Journal, Barron's, Fortune, Business Week* or *Forbes* as well as the trade periodicals of their own business. They are smart enough to make many of their own investment decisions and see no reason to pay exorbitant commissions to brokerage house registered representatives just for being their order taker.

I am so proud of the American people, who in the last two decades have become so well educated in money matters. The consumer movement has helped create a nation of wiser people that cannot readily be hookwinked or fed with poppycock. As the recent *Business Week* article flatly stated, the insurance industry's customers are "rebelling." And, in my opinion, it's not a moment too soon.

There are some indications, however, that the more enlightened members of the life insurance establishment are beginning to see the light. In a recent article in *Best's Review*, insurance consultant and writer Dave Goodwin presented some interesting views. Goodwin's article was an update of a 1973 article entitled "The Life Insurance Industry Must Change Its Image to Consumers," which addressed the industry's image problems and the reasons behind them. In that early article. Goodwin declared,

> "This is how the industry has hurt itself. It has prospered in its own inbred world for so long that it is too slow to recognize festering problems. However, the forces of change are breathing hot, and we are providing their best ammunition."

His conclusion in the 1989 article, entitled "Here We Go Again," was that many of the industry's problems had not been addressed and that, indeed, strong, positive steps were necessary to prevent further disintegration of the industry's reputation and profits. Observing the fact that, historically, every 30 years has seen investigation and scandal in the insurance industry, Goodwin declared, "Our 30 year cycle is due to crest, and if it does so, now it will be in the atmosphere of an intense consumerist mood much broader and deeper than any before."

Goodwin is quite right. The entire life insurance industry made the identical mistakes that the U.S. automobile industry made; they totally ignored giving the American people a product they could afford, that they needed, and that they desired. Little did the managements of these great industries understand that during the past twenty years of runaway inflation most Americans could not afford what they were trying to sell them. In the case of the life insurance industry they persisted in trying to sell high cost cash value life insurance. In the auto industry, they kept on jacking up the prices in spite of the inferior products they were peddling. The life companies went much further than Detroit in bilking people with inferior products.

As the consumer becomes more aware about insurance products, the role of the salesman may be forced to change as well.

The insurance agent can be especially useful in arranging life insurance protection. But he must be totally aware of low cost term insurance and investing the difference. Unfortunately too many still have their eyes on cash value life insurance and high commissions.

The big reason is that the life insurance market is extremely confused and chaotic. In spite of the monopolistic practices of the big establishment companies, or perhaps because of this roguery and the incompetence of so many persons in the business, the range of policies and the variations in premium prices from company to company for practically identical policies are well nigh incredible. Price variations for the same products can run to 100 percent.

Nevertheless, if the typical insurance agent wants to

continue to make a decent living, he is going to have to adapt to the winds of change. He (or she) is going to have to recover from the brainwashing he was subjected to by the establishment companies during early training.

Specifically, the agent must learn to sell a lot more term (death) protection at much cheaper premiums because that is what people want and need now, and the agent will have to get used to much more modest commissions than he is accustomed to getting on the whole life cash value he was taught to sell. In the future, the agent must depend for a living on a lot of reasonable fees for offering a fairly wide assortment of financial services to customers. Those who don't do this may find themselves out of business. The industry as a whole must learn these lessons, as well. As Goodwin states, "The life policy should never have been sold as the only financial product a consumer would ever need. Similarly, life industry leaders must understand that they represent a business, not a religion."

As we've seen in examples throughout this book, the motive of the establishment life companies in trying to preserve yesterday is obvious: It's greed.

The addition of cash values to whole life insurance was originally a sales gimmick because life insurance was hard to sell in its early years for a variety of reasons. The company managers soon realized that cash values were a potential gold mine, people easily could be deluded into paying much more exorbitant prices for them than they already were paying for expensive ordinary whole life insurance.

The exorbitant premiums they obtained for the combination of whole life insurance and cash values (which gave policyholders the illusion that they were accumulating savings) brought the companies an enormous flow of cash to invest in real estate, bonds, stocks and even more profitable things. The life insurance business really did became a gold mine.

But even in that climate of a hundred and fifty years ago there were persons wanting to buy life insurance protection who knew the correct odds and had sufficient influence in high places to compel the companies to sell them life insurance protection for relatively short fixed terms at greatly reduced premium prices.

Even though they had to yield to this pressure, the companies succeeded for about a century in keeping this term insurance business secret from the public and even from their own agents and most of their employees.

When the success of group insurance accelerated a demand for cheap individual term life policies, the establishment companies fought ferociously to stem this demand. They used strategies too numerous to describe here to cool the demand for term insurance and resorted to every variety of false propaganda about the supposed virtues of whole life cash value insurance. But new companies were founded to write individual term life insurance and ultimately the big establishment companies had to start offering individual term policies. But they continue to drag their feet in the term market, putting arbitrary floors on the face amounts of term policies in order to price them out of most people's reach and punishing agents in various ways for selling them.

They are still striving furiously to hold back the dawn and delude or compel people to buy their expensive whole life cash value policies. What is worse, they are employing all kinds of propaganda and chicanery to persuade older policyholders to hang on to old whole life policies whose cash values and face values have been so eroded by inflation that they no longer are worth what they cost.

From my vantage point, I insist that it is no longer possible for the average American, regardless of how much money he or she makes, to buy anything other than term (death) insurance. After all, even a $50,000 a year income, after federal, state and city taxes and the most horrendous tax of all, inflation, will just about cover the bare necessities of life.

The better informed segments of the American public began recognizing the superiority of term life insurance so much that, by the early 1970's, about half of all new life insurance being sold was term, either group or individual.

At last the establishment companies began to see the handwriting on the wall and expressed their consternation at the way things were going in the aforementioned 1974 *Trend Report*. This report recommended a lot of changes, but the changes all were designed to preserve the profits of the company insiders. Nobody else was to be protected. New products were to be introduced, but they were designed only to shave costs, not to improve service to customers or give people really adequate protection against early death. The public was still to be damned.

Above all else was put the determination not to do anything for some one hundred fifty million Americans who were stuck with badly eroded whole life, cash value life insurance bought many years ago. Every effort would continue to be made to get the state commissioners to enforce even more sternly the rules preventing insurance agents from trying to help people to replace the deteriorated whole life, cash value policies with cheaper term policies offering many times as much protection, and to invest the premium money thus saved in something that would bring them real income and real savings.

This situation is, in many ways, a national disgrace!

What is good for new life insurance buyers ought to be even better for the holders of outmoded policies designed under the archaic and predatory strategies and outdated mortality tables of the past! Nearly all that whole life insurance ought to be replaced now by vastly larger amounts of reasonably priced term insurance, giving the policyholders in their prime years five to ten times as much protection for the same or even less money. These policyholders then should be encouraged to invest the money saved on premiums in mutual funds and other investment vehicles that will bring them real return.

But selling replacement life insurance is a highly ticklish and controversial matter. It is regulated by law in every state and these regulations are for the most part archaic. Their enforcement by state insurance commissioners often is rigorous because of the pressure the commissioners get from the establishment companies to curb replacement. A lot of red tape must be complied with and much costly paperwork done by the agent who wants to help people improve their lot by replacing high premium whole life cash value policies with sensibly priced term that provides real protection against early death.

The newer, more innovative life companies and marketing organizations that specialize in providing term insurance must cope with these archaic regulations and how to comply with them and still carry out the replacement transactions successfully for the betterment of the public at large. Because few companies today have mastered distribution systems well enough to be able to provide reasonably-priced term insurance to mainstream America, it is still difficult to find companies that promote the sale of term insurance only, but they do exist. Finding a company that actively sells term insurance may take a little more effort, but the diligent consumer will find that the search for such a company will more than "pay off" in perhaps thousands of dollars saved on insurance costs, as well as adequate insurance coverage for their families.

If the huge sums saved on the amount of premiums paid on term insurance in comparison with the cost of whole life cash value insurance are prudently invested in plans that are compounded, a side fund will accumulate that is much larger than either the cash values or the death benefit (including the so-called "dividends) in a whole life policy. And, of course, the beneficiary of a term policy will still get the death benefit settlement if he/she dies while the term policy is in force.

In addition to enjoying real financial protection throughout the prime years, the family that buys term insurance and invests the money saved on premiums with reasonable prudence will come out way ahead of those who let themselves be deluded into believing life insurance is a good way to save.

Nearly all those 150 million Americans who still have outdated life insurance policies need to learn the lesson that there is no such thing as a need for permanent life insurance. As I have mentioned earlier, almost everyone's need for life insurance protection diminishes after their children are grown and it's generally foolish to keep on paying for maximum protection in the twilight years.

The tragedy is that millions of persons are going without adequate protection in their prime years, risking hardship for their children, and paying the establishment companies' exorbitant premiums for smallish amounts of protection they won't even need.

It is in order to hang on to these undeserved and antisocial profits that the establishment companies are striving so hard to preserve yesterday.

Yet it may no longer be possible. According to *Business Week*, "the once-tranquil world of insurance is in turmoil. Instead of the most ignored industry in America, it has become perhaps the most reviled." The windfall profits made at the expense of the uninformed consumer may well be a thing of "yesterday" for the insurance industry.

It's time to drag them into today and force them to face up to tomorrow.

Yes! Let us all *tell yesterday goodby.*

Epilogue

IN THE LAST CHAPTER OF THIS BOOK, I talked about the latest article in *Business Week* magazine, which espoused many of the same views that were presented in the original version of *How Your Life Insurance Policies Rob You.* I am no longer as lonely as I used to be in carrying common-sense philosophies to the American people about their "money matters."

Since that time, literally hundreds of newspaper and magazine articles, radio programs, and television segments have discussed those very things that I started to talk about ten years ago. These many presentations, along with this book, have been educating consumers as to what they should do for themselves and their families to ensure the financial freedom required to live in dignity, retire in dignity, and die in dignity.

The free enterprise system in America is the greatest in the world. But that same freedom of action that grants us so many opportunities also leaves open many loopholes for the frauds in all professions to sneak through. Earlier I

mentioned the surgical profession, and the many unnecessary operations that are performed each year on
unsuspecting patients. I need not mention the unnecessary
dental work as well, or how often other professionals in
the accounting and legal fields give the real "zing" to their
clients.

Insurance professionals are no different. When the
jaundiced eyes of the salesperson are on the commission
dollar and not on what's good for the client, his or her
actions are all too often less than exemplary.

Millions have already seen the light, and I know that
as we enter the decade of the 1990's, heading for the 21st
century, millions upon millions more will right the
wrongs that the insurance industry has done to them. It is
my fervent hope that this message will go a long way to
continue to educate, to continue to foster debate, and to
continue to arouse concern in the life insurance industry
and increase competition so that the old caveat, "Let the
buyer beware," will *absolutely* be changed to "Let the
competition beware."

So often, victims of financial abuse in this country
bring to my mind the unfortunate victims of rape, of
whom so few come forward that we don't really know the
actual number who have been harmed for life. Financial
rape victims are no different. Very few come forward;
they just suffer in silence, knowing that they have been
taken. But the psychological toll on these people for their
poor planning and poor personal financial
management—causing such things as divorce, meager living conditions, and many other serious problems—is a
reality in America today.

More and more, life insurance companies have
started to enact the "invest the difference" portion of my

theories by issuing tax-deferred annuities and setting up mutual funds. But they have not taken that important step forward that would involve educating their salespeople about lower-priced term insurance, which allows a "difference" to invest. Setting up a mutual fund is a good "first step" for an established company, but what good will it do if the company executives don't instruct their salespeople to "do the job" the *right way* for the American people?

I have been accused by executives and high officers of insurance companies and trade associations of upsetting the industry status quo. To that I say, "Amen!" That so-called status quo was in desperate need of an upset, if the American people are to take control of their financial destinies.

It's time for action to be taken. As I reflect on all this, I am thinking about the title and theme of my next book, *The Unscrewing of America.*

The fight by and for American consumers goes on. And it will be won.